D0915647

CORPORATE ARCHIVES
AND HISTORY:
Making the Past Work

CORPORATE ARCHIVES AND HISTORY:
Making the Past Work

Edited by
Arnita A. Jones
and
Philip L. Cantelon

KRIEGER PUBLISHING COMPANY
MALABAR, FLORIDA
1993

Original Edition 1993

Printed and Published by
KRIEGER PUBLISHING COMPANY
KRIEGER DRIVE
MALABAR, FL 32950

Library of Congress Cataloging-in-Publication Data

Corporate archives and history : making the past work / [edited] by Arnita A. Jones and
    Philip L. Cantelon.
        p.   cm.
    ISBN 0-89464-353-3 (acid-free paper)
    1. Business records.   2. Corporations—Archives.   I. Jones, Arnita A.   II. Cantelon,
Philip L. (Philip Louis),   1940–
HF5736.C63   1992
026'.3387--dc20   91-46918
                                                                                         CIP

10   9   8   7   6   5   4   3   2

CONTENTS

EDITORS

Arnita A. Jones is currently executive secretary of the Organization of American Historians and a member of the Board of Directors of History Associates Incorporated. A former program officer for Planning and Assessment Studies at the National Endowment for the Humanities and director of the National Coordinating Committee for the Promotion of History, Jones also has organized and led seminars on corporate archives and history at several colleges and universities. She holds Ph.D. and M.A. degrees in history from Emory University, and also has served as chair of the National Council on Public History and as a member of the Council of the Society for History in the Federal Government.

Philip L. Cantelon has been president of History Associates Incorporated since it was established in 1981. A member of the Oral History Association for fifteen years and formerly executive director of the National Council on Public History, Dr. Cantelon also was a founder and secretary-treasurer of the Society for History in the Federal Government. A graduate of Dartmouth College and Indiana University, he taught contemporary American history at Williams College and has supervised and conducted extensive oral history and archive programs for several corporate history projects, including the Consolidated Edison Company of New York, Texas Instruments, Rainier Bancorporation, the Bank of New York, and MCI Communications Corporation. He also is the co-author of a history of the Three-Mile Island nuclear accident, *Crisis Contained*, and *The American Atom*.

PREFACE

Why should a modern corporation divert scarce resources to the collection and maintenance of historical records? Who are the users of business archives? Are there professional standards that apply to the employment of corporate archivists? What is the best way for an organization to go about developing an archives? What steps should be taken to protect records in the event of a disaster or emergency? Are there issues or problems unique to the work of an archivist or historian in a business setting? What are the implications of the increasing use of electronic records? Is a company better off to have developed an archives or, rather, to have developed no records policy at all in the event of litigation proceedings?

For years no ready or reliable answers were available to these and other questions relating to the place of business records in American society, despite the fact that changes in the structure of American corporations have increasingly eroded the ability of those organizations to rely on individual memories for guidance in contemporary policy and decision making. Forces are at work, however, to alter these patterns.

For whatever reasons, the number of corporate archives grew significantly in the 1960s and 1970s. Although that rate of growth has tapered off somewhat, and in a few cases important archival programs have been discontinued, a critical mass of experience is now available from which to draw. Corporate decision makers who have become convinced of the value of maintaining a sound and accurate historical record, either as a part of their public information programs or integrated into their internal decision-making processes, currently have a variety of models to observe, from financial institutions to service companies to manufacturing concerns. Today we have also an experienced group of highly professional business archivists who can and do provide advice to organizations considering an archival program or to individuals considering a career in the field.

The increasing professionalization of business archives has been a key factor in the evolution of the modern corporate archives. Once an anomaly, today the skilled business archivist or historian is a part of an increasingly self-conscious peer group. Cognizant of heightened public and academic interest in their work, these professionals are increasingly aware of the need to balance responsible public inquiry into their organizations' records with management's long-term needs.

The collection of essays which follows has more than one audience in view. Managers in corporations who have responsibility for records are a primary audience. With them in mind we have provided examples of different ways in which companies have developed archival programs, how these can be managed in a cost effective manner, and how they can be fully utilized by different segments of the organization. We also believe that this volume can serve as a supplement to the curriculum in archives and public history programs in higher education institutions, where students considering careers in this area can receive an introduction to the field. Finally, we hope that the modern corporate archives—professionally administered, responsive to the needs of management, and accessible ultimately to the public and to serious and responsible scholars—will create a better understanding of the role of business in American life.

The idea for this book evolved out of a series of seminars on corporate archives and history, organized by the editors over the past several years. In conjunction with local universities or schools of business, these programs covered a wide range of themes pertinent to the establishment of an archives facility for the collection and use of historical records and analyses in a corporate setting. Participants explored ways in which some corporations are increasingly using their histories to support community and public relations programs, marketing efforts, employee and management training courses, and corporate planning efforts. Historical materials discussed included artifacts, past advertising copy, and corporate publications such as newsletters and other internal communications, along with oral histories and more traditional historical sources such as board of directors' meeting minutes, executive correspondence, legal briefs, business plans, and other policy documents. We also probed the critical relationship between archives and records management and the need for proper administration of both areas to create effective procedures for preserving the historical record at an affordable cost.

We have attempted to keep the lessons from these seminars in mind when selecting materials for this volume. *Corporate Archives and History: Making the Past Work* is designed to offer a basic overview of the value of corporate history and to present a number of case studies that can assist corporations in developing an archival/records management/historical program best suited for their needs. All the contributors are professional archivists, records managers, or historians. All have extensive experience in working in or with the corporate world. We believe that their knowledge and ideas will prove valuable to those faced with mounting costs of storing records, with meeting demands to locate old documents, and with preserving critical elements of a company's past.

This volume is part of a continuing series of publications sponsored by the National Council of Public History, a professional organization representing many historians and archivists who apply their skills outside the academy in many different kinds of settings. We would like to thank Barbara J. Howe, whose idea and determination inaugurated this series, and Mary Roberts, our editor at Krieger, who has demonstrated both patience and pleasure in seeing this work through completion. These are virtues of the ideal editor. Of course, nothing could have been accomplished without the timely contributions of the authors represented in the book. Singling out one or two would be unfair to the rest. We thank you all. Kara Hamm cheerfully typed the manuscript in Bloomington, and Judy Bressler-Saad performed the East coast typing chores, while Lucie Usher served as copy editor. Laurie Cadigan Peterson, Robert W. Pomeroy, and Noel Stowe commented on the manuscript and offered ideas for improvement. Everyone involved made this group effort enjoyable as well as stimulating. Lastly, we would like to thank our spouses, Landis Jones and Eileen McGuckian, for delighting in the work with us. Or at least being polite enough to say so.

Donn C. Neal joined the National Archives and Records Administration in October 1990 as director of Congressional and External Affairs. Prior to that appointment, he served as executive director of the Society of American Archivists (1986–1990), executive director of the Pittsburgh Council on Higher Education (1981–1986), vice president of the Great Lakes Colleges Association (1976–1981), and assistant professor of history at Elmira College (1967–1976). Neal received his B.A. from Alma College and his M.A. and Ph.D. from the University of Michigan. He is the author of The World Beyond the Hudson: Alfred E. Smith and National Politics, 1918–1928 *and editor of* Consortia and Interinstitutional Cooperation.

INTRODUCTION

Donn C. Neal

A good archives is good business. An organization profits when its records having lasting fiscal, legal, evidential, historical, and administrative value are preserved and managed so that the essential information in them can be brought to bear upon the organization's current needs and future planning. This is so whether the organization is a university, a government agency, a religious body, or a corporation, but it is especially true for an organization that is dedicated to business principles.

An organization is shaped by the past more than it realizes, and an archives enables it to transform information from the institution's past into an asset for better management. Unfortunately, many corporations today are losing their past. Vital information is disappearing at an alarming rate; it is not recorded at all, it is strewn through a mass of routine documentation, it is mistakenly discarded, or it disappears because of a lack of proper care.

Like organizations everywhere, corporations are in danger of being overwhelmed by growing mountains of information: executive correspondence and memoranda, sales and distribution reports, contracts and agreements, engineering plans and product designs, and statistical and personnel records. In addition, the formats on which information is created and maintained have proliferated: films and magnetic tapes, microforms and optical disks. All these have become as important as paper in storing valuable information. Careful management of information is a must, and sophisticated media demand professional care if the information they record is to function as a key resource.

While corporations are being overwhelmed by a burgeoning volume of records, they are, paradoxically, too often unable to locate truly vital information. Without an adequate archival program, important records may be misplaced; without proper preservation measures, many valuable documents will literally self-destruct; without precautions, an unanticipated disaster can wipe out irreplaceable information. Even when the

1

records have been kept, and eventually can be located, the lack of an effective archival program may make it difficult for the corporation to respond promptly and accurately not only to its own information needs but to legitimate outside queries—from government agencies, consumers, and the media.

Corporations will grow increasingly unable to solve these challenges without an efficient, comprehensive archival records program. In such a program, current and inactive records are well organized and those with permanent value (generally, no more than 2 to 5 percent) are identified, segregated, and carefully maintained in an adequate, centralized facility in a manner that will both protect them and facilitate reference and research.

Good decisions are based on good information; better management results from better archives. Informed by a more complete historical perspective, managers make better decisions about policies, initiatives, strategies, and the overall direction of the corporation. Just as a physician finds a patient history invaluable in making a diagnosis and in determining treatment, and as an attorney studies legal precedents and previous court decisions, a corporate manager examines the corporation's record of actions and responses before making a decision. Ready access to board minutes, technical reports, advertising materials, product development files, plant and facility records, and other key forms of information is a vital managerial tool.

Memories are short. People come and go, particularly in today's business climate of acquisitions, mergers, and takeovers, and with the high turnover in managers that the business world experiences. Information in a corporation's archives can enable new employees, including new managers, to understand the distinctive aspects and special ethos of the company and its way of doing business. Professionally managed records can help them to gain a knowledge of the company's governing policies and the direction that it is pursuing. By studying what marketing strategies led to high growth in sales, what corporate executives said about a key topic, what kinds of research stimulated new product development, or what investors were told during a particularly troublesome time, today's corporate managers can comprehend better their current challenges, rediscover successful responses, and avoid painful mistakes.

First and foremost, then, a corporate archives helps a business to understand itself: how it got where it is today, its strengths and shortcomings, and its role within its sphere of operations. Archival information can show how the corporation has evolved, how it has developed new products and services, how it has responded to the challenges of adversity and the opportunities of prosperity, and how it has related to larger forces in its environment. By documenting the changing nature of its structure, technology, and strategies, the corporation can better understand its capabilities, exploit its potential, and avoid miscalculations.

Ready access to needed information, besides giving the corporation a valuable strategic and managerial advantage, assures the protection of its interests and property rights, both physical and intellectual. Archival records can help to prove ownership of an idea, design, patent, trademark, or technology. They can show contractual rights and document licensing agreements. Blueprints and engineering reports can help the company to defend itself in liability cases. Financial records—the cost of acquisitions, for instance—can demonstrate the corporation's financial standing in tax cases.

Archival records, moreover, assist the corporation in projecting a positive image of itself and in creating good will. Information about the corporation can build identity and loyalty among employees and can prove useful in orientation and training programs. These records also help the corporation in dealing with its various publics: stockholders and investors, consumers, neighbors, the media, and government officials. By documenting key milestones, anniversaries, special events, and other aspects of the corporation's past, archival records can serve as a foundation for public relations and marketing campaigns that seek to influence thinking about the corporation and its products and services. Exhibits, publications, advertising campaigns, stockholders reports, and a corporate museum are examples of the conscious use of archival materials for image making. Similarly, information from the archives can make a contribution to case studies and other educational materials dealing with the history and development of business practices in the United States, and so also help to shape knowledge and understanding of the role that the business has played.

A corporate archives saves money as well. By assisting in the separation of information that is truly valuable from the mass of documentation that is not, the corporate archivist can help the firm to keep less than it had kept before. Less storage means lower costs— and less lost time searching for important information. Winnowing the routine and duplicate information from what is maintained produces further savings. Being able to produce the necessary documentation also can prevent costly losses in lawsuits, tax cases, and liability judgments.

The archivist also will help to control legitimate internal and external access to corporate records, especially those containing sensitive, confidential, or proprietary information. If the corporation sponsors or permits scholarly research, the archivist will work with researchers to locate relevant information. Finally, the archivist can be a key helper when mandatory outside audits and reviews take place, relieving other corporate officials of an unfamiliar role.

Thus, a wide range of corporate departments—from human relations to legal to marketing to strategic planning—benefits from a corporate archives. An archives is not a storehouse of dusty, unused records. Neither is it an altruistic gift to future researchers. Nor is it a monument to corporate ego. Instead, it is an asset to better management—a practical, living instrument through which the corporation can marshall the information it produces and collects, can gain ready access to this information as needed, and can use the information to achieve its corporate goals.

Ideally, a corporate archivist participates in corporate decisions about how information is created, maintained, and managed within the organization. The archivist works with records creators to ensure that information is in fact securely stored, and with records managers to distinguish between the vast bulk of records that can be systematically disposed of and the small minority that has lasting value. A trained, professional archivist brings special skills to the tasks of appraising the potential long-term value of the information that the corporation creates, initiating preservation measures, reformatting the information as required, and then arranging and cataloging what should be saved so that the information can be put to use. Using his or her expertise in understanding how an organization creates and holds its records, the archivist can help others find and use the information contained in the corporate archives.

Establishment of an archives often attracts "lost" materials that may have been stored in a corporate building or tucked away in a former employee's attic. The archivist also may seek out additional information for the corporation's archives, especially through an oral history program, in order to fill gaps in the record or to supplement written records with unique personal recollections or insights. The archivist also will cooperate with fellow professionals in other organizations, including other corporations, in order to raise the standard of practice in the field and the level of awareness of the archives' value.

Hundreds of American businesses and corporations have discovered the many benefits of a soundly based, well run archival program. This number has increased in recent years, and corporate archivists have become a major interest group within the profession as a whole. Taken together, these corporate archives enlighten those who seek to understand the development of this country's business sector, just as they enable decision makers within those businesses and corporations to understand their own firms. America's corporate sector is a key part of its cultural, economic, and political character, and corporate archives constitute an indispensable tool for comprehending and interpreting the role that corporations have played in this nation's development. At the same time, these corporate archives help their parent organizations to strengthen themselves so that they can not only survive but thrive in today's business climate.

Writing in *History of the Idea of Progress*, Robert Nisbet observed that without the past we are "condemned to a form of isolation in time that easily becomes self-destructive." In meeting the enormous challenges of global competition, new technologies, and an economy of scarcities, American corporations cannot afford the luxury of an "isolation in time." This volume will contribute to a better understanding of the value that corporate archival programs have, both to their corporations and to others, and so it is a welcome addition to the archival literature.

PART I
GETTING STARTED: RECENT CASE STUDIES ON THE DEVELOPMENT OF BUSINESS ARCHIVES

GETTING STARTED: RECENT CASE STUDIES ON THE DEVELOPMENT OF BUSINESS ARCHIVES

Archives are not as yet routine in the corporate world. While any organization must have some form of records management, explicit or not, the existence of archival programs cannot be taken for granted. Occasionally, a manufacturing company realizes the marketing potential of its past as a way of invoking nostalgia for an older line of products, or a financial institution discovers the value of historical connections in creating a sense of stability. A number of corporate archives are the product of anniversaries, but others seem to have resulted from emergencies—a crisis in which key records had to be rescued. And as the reasons for their existence vary so, too, do the nature and scope of specific business archives—as well as their mission and place in the organizational structure.

There are, however, a number of common problems organizations must confront as they set about to establish an archives. Included in this section are several case studies which will illustrate the problems that must be addressed by archivists or those responsible for developing a formal program for care of permanent records. The case studies chosen for this section represent several different kinds of businesses—from one of the nation's oldest financial institutions to an entertainment company to a high-tech organization founded in the post-World War II era.

The first selection provides an overview of the development of corporate archives in this century. Philip F. Mooney in "The Practice of History in Corporate America: Business Archives in the United States" notes that different types of companies are likely to use and keep different kinds of records, a fact that heavily influences their decision as to the nature of the archives they may wish to establish. He stresses, as do the other authors in this section, the need for those responsible for historical records to think through very carefully their role in the larger organization and to take care to maintain management support of their work.

Nancy M. Merz and Sally L. Merryman tell different parts of the story of Texas Instruments' relatively new archives. Like so many others, this company considered its records unimportant until faced with the imminent loss of institutional memory through the retirement or death of its founders. Solving the immediate problem by calling in a group of historical consultants, Texas Instruments still faced the staggering tasks of locating key permanent records among thousands of cubic feet of storage and of identifying fugitive material in active office areas, personal collec-

tions of executives, and international installations. Merz, an archivist with
History Associates Incorporated, describes how she and her team method-
ically went about establishing a mission for the archives, locating and
processing documents, developing a data retrieval system, and establishing the role of the program within the company.

Merryman focuses on the process of transforming the archives from a
discreet operation managed by outside consultants to a full-fledged unit
of Texas Instruments. Noting the tension between the continued need for
surveying and processing records, and serving the company's ever-
expanding information needs, she stresses the importance of corporate
archivists' willingness to perform the latter function. Continuing to grow,
the archives at Texas Instruments is taking advantage of new storage and
data retrieval technologies. Archives personnel have begun to research
and write histories for both commemorative and policy purposes, and also
to develop museum exhibits and videos.

No book on corporate archives would be complete without a description
of the work of Harold P. Anderson and his predecessors at Wells Fargo &
Company. Perhaps the best known corporate archives and history program in the country, Wells Fargo's operation provides an excellent illustration of the way in which a company's age and range of services dictate the
nature of its archives. But the history program of this venerable banking
institution is more than the romantic exploitation of its stagecoach em-
blem. Anderson shows us how the archives provides support for the
information needs of many departments within the company as well as
those of scholars and others in the community. He stresses, as do Merz and
Merryman, the complex nature of documentation in the modern corporation which has often experienced literally dozens of mergers and acquisitions.

The problems of dealing with a complex corporate genealogy are not
limited to older institutions. Edward L. Galvin of The Aerospace Corporation had to deal with similar problems in developing an archives in a high-
tech corporation scarcely thirty years old. A part of library services, the
fledgling archives at Aerospace is less influenced by the needs of public
information or marketing personnel and more integrated with the company's own research needs. The steps Galvin outlines as critical to the
establishment of an archives are nonetheless similar to those followed at
Texas Instruments. Both provide an excellent checklist of measures which
should be included in any comprehensive archives development plan.

Paula M. Sigman's story from The Walt Disney Archives provides an
illustration of the dangers facing even a mature archives in the event of a
merger or change of management. Roughly a quarter-century old, with a
constituency of thousands of staff who had been through the archives
"Traditions" course as well as countless fans and collectors outside the
organization, the Disney archives still faced a major threat with the
installation of a new cost-conscious management team. Sigman's story of
how the archives staff developed a creative and ultimately successful
response to this danger should be required reading for all organizational
archivists.

Philip F. Mooney has managed the Archives Department at The Coca-Cola Company since 1977. Prior to joining Coca-Cola, he was an archivist at Syracuse University and at The Balch Institute for Ethnic Studies in Philadelphia. Mooney has served as an instructor at ten Business Archives Workshops sponsored by the Society of American Archivists and has chaired the Business Archives section of the Society. His articles on the development and management of business archives have appeared in Public History: An Introduction *(1986),* Researcher's Guide to Archival and Regional History Collections *(1988),* Drexel Library Quarterly, American Archivist, Proceedings of the Sewanee Economics Symposium, *and the* Business History Bulletin. *He also is an advisor to the oral history program at the Center for Advertising History at the Smithsonian Institution.*

THE PRACTICE OF HISTORY IN CORPORATE AMERICA: BUSINESS ARCHIVES IN THE UNITED STATES

Philip F. Mooney

About 2000 B.C. a guild of Assyrian merchants established a central depository for the records of their commercial activities, marking the establishment of the first business history collection. Family mercantile records, banking documents, and notarial files later became useful resources for the study of commercial development, but the more widespread acquisition of business records for scholarly use did not occur until the early 20th century when public archival agencies throughout western Europe began to establish regional centers for the collection of business records. Not until the establishment of the Business History Society at Harvard University in 1925 and the pioneering collecting work of the Harvard Business School in the same period did American institutions begin to regard business history as a legitimate academic pursuit. The establishment of graduate business schools and the resulting demand for primary research materials ultimately led to the formation of strong business collections at major academic libraries throughout the United States.[1]

The formation and development of internal archival units within corporate organizational structures is an even more recent phenomenon. Germany's Krupp Company established the first business archives in 1905 when that firm was preparing a formal history. Almost four decades later, the initial American program began when the Firestone Tire and Rubber Company hired archivist William Overman to ensure that valuable histori-

Reprinted with permission. Barbara J. Howe and Emory L. Kemp, eds., *Public History: An Introduction* (Malabar, Florida: Robert E. Krieger Publishing Company, 1986.)

cal records were not destroyed as part of a records management program. Still, the Firestone example did not stir many other corporations to follow their lead. By 1960 only 51 companies reported archives of any sort, and only a handful employed a full-time archivist."[2] In many firms librarians performed an archival function, while in others the records manager had the responsibility for determining which records to class as historical.

While archival development was slow, history was not entirely neglected in corporate America. A 1943 study conducted by the American Association of Museums identified 80 businesses that supported internal museum programs. Cost justified for their public relations value and for their utility as a visible history of patent, engineering, and trademark use, they generally developed at manufacturing firms that had prided themselves on a tradition of excellence. As with existing archival units, many of the collections were administered by retirees or "well-intentioned" librarians.[3]

Most of the museums identified in the AAM study occupied a small parcel of space in the corporate headquarters with limited public access. The skills of the historian manifested themselves only in the selection of the objects to be displayed and in the development of related publications. In many cases the museum and archival functions gradually merged, accounting to some degree for the rapid growth that has occurred over the last quarter century in business archives.

In surveys conducted by the Society of American Archivists, corporations claiming archives numbered 133 in 1969, 196 in 1975, and over 200 by 1980, ranging from the single file drawer of newspaper clippings and ephemera to well-organized historical units. The surveys did not attempt to make qualitative evaluations of the respondents. A number of popular business publications, summarizing survey data, have mistakenly interpreted these figures as signaling an emerging frontier for historians in the future.[4] In fact, while significant growth has occurred within the field, only 60 full-time archivists were identified in the same survey.[5]

The five dozen corporations supporting internal archival departments represent a cross-section of American businesses including consumer product companies like Coca-Cola, Sears, Procter and Gamble, Kraft, Weyerhaeuser, Corning, Walt Disney, and General Mills; financial institutions such as Chase Manhattan, the New York Stock Exchange, Wells Fargo, Nationwide Insurance, Bank of America and Cigna; high-tech industries like United Technologies, Control Data, Mitre, and Texas Instruments; John Deere and International Harvester representing the transportation industry; and institutions like the *Los Angeles Times*, Colonial Williamsburg, and the Educational Testing Service, which stand alone within their industry segments. While the diversity of this selective listing is apparent, all of these institutions are large, well-established entities which can easily support historical services as part of the corporate overhead. Smaller firms can rarely rationalize such expenditures unless they can be linked to their informational or records management functions. In such instances, the archives is usually positioned as a smaller element of a corporate library system or records program.

The rationale for the establishment of an archives can differ dramatically among corporations, but major reasons include the celebration of an anniversary or special event, the production of a corporate history, the needs of internal departments for immediate historical information, pending litigation and/or the specific directive of a chief executive officer. The programs at Wells Fargo, Chase Manhattan, and Control Data began when management recognized that an organized historical collection would make the decision-making process easier because they would have access to the records of past management practices. At American Telephone and Telegraph, the process of producing a major historical study stimulated the formation of the archives, while a Canadian anniversary celebration and the resulting search for packaging samples motivated General Mills to the same decision. At Coca-Cola, the need for documentation in a 1941 trademark case underscored the need for the formal maintenance of a historical collection. Regardless of the initial impetus, successful programs are those that have clearly positioned their long-term functions as relevant contributors to stated corporate strategies.

In some cases business leaders, hoping to preserve the record of their accomplishments, have initiated archival programs by executive fiat. With such a limited statement of purpose, those archives serve the same function as pyramids for the pharaohs. Without a life of their own or broad-based internal support, they are doomed to extinction when a new management group with a philosophy oriented toward a different goal assumes control of the firm.

Unless management clearly perceives the archives as a vital, progressive, contributory information center that renders direct support to the business, its long-term existence is unlikely. While historical consultant George David Smith has suggested that corporations are "hungry" for history and that studies of past actions are "therapeutic" for industries facing hard decisions in times of great turmoil, Deborah Gardner, archivist of the New York Stock Exchange, pinpointed the more basic concern facing practicing archivists when she observed that the corporate sector does not readily perceive itself as having a historical function.[6] To the degree that the archivist can identify the benefits of history to the parent body the more successful and secure the archival program will become.

The organizational structures most prevalent in American corporations position the archives within an administrative services group, in a public relations department, or in the office of the corporate secretary. Like other organizational units, the form and positioning of the archives strongly reflect the business function. Companies with a strong consumer products orientation often perceive the archives as a valuable public relations vehicle, while financial institutions may find that the office of the secretary may require more frequent access to historical files for the completion of important projects. Administrative placement offers even more functional flexibility ranging from strategic planning to centralized information management.

All of these structures can operate equally well provided that the

Figure 1. Protecting the historical trademark is an important function of the archives at
The Coca-Cola Company. *Courtesy of The Coca-Cola Corporation.*

archivist has access to decision makers. Ideally, the archivist should have
the title of department head, manage an independent budget, and report
directly to a corporate officer. The archivist should be able to communicate to senior management on a regular basis and to receive feedback on
programs in a timely fashion. The desired objective is to reduce the
number of layers through which information must travel.

Rather than simply serving as the corporate memory, the archives must
render valuable, practical services to business that could not be easily
secured from other sources. The functions of the office must be directed
toward the achievement of goals and objectives that are positive, pro-
active, and consistent with the corporate culture of the institution. To
accomplish this, the archivist must truly be a practitioner of applied
history, and ongoing programs must withstand the harsh empirical testing
of skeptical business associates. While continuing to exercise the analytical
techniques of the historian, the corporate archivist also must possess
strong communications skills to properly position the department, its
purpose, and activities. The tenure decision in the business world is not
restricted to the individual; it is expanded to include his organization.
"Produce or perish" is substituted for the traditional "publish or perish."

Figure 2. Historical materials can be an important part of employee training and public relations programs. *Courtesy of The Coca-Cola Corporation.*

Archives do not exist in a corporate vacuum; they demand relationships with other departments and functions. These linkages expand bases of operation, allowing the archivist to manage historical resources and to achieve results that are both understandable and measurable. Ties to areas such as marketing, advertising, public relations, human resources, training, legal, strategic planning, stockholder relations, research and development, and publications establish a strong user network for cooperative program development.

Marketing plans today are based on programs that have succeeded in past decades. The glitter and packaging surrounding the promotion may change, but its essential shape and content hardly vary. An office that can supply detailed data on previous business achievements can help to plot new campaigns that hold the promise of similar results. Similarly, an analysis of disappointing or disastrous promotions can alert marketing strategists to the perils of poorly structured programs. Sales promotion files, packaging and advertising samples, sales aids, and financial reports help companies like General Foods, Sears, Kraft, and Ford to capitalize on successful ideas while avoiding the pitfalls that caused other campaigns to falter.

In a highly technological age, complex corporate organizations and highly mobile work forces have combined to eliminate heritage and tradition as factors in the formation of corporate policy. The effects of merger, acquisition, litigation, and records management also have contributed to corporate memory shortages. As a counterweight to these trends, the archives can provide access to the policies, standards, philosophies, and environment that influenced previous decisions and can recapture critical strategic information that helped shape the business.

Wells Fargo Bank offers a unique case study in applied history on the corporate level through its support of over a dozen members of the archival staff who routinely prepare detailed analytical reports on financial policies and procedures and publish an impressive series of monographs on regional banking history. The archives also staffs three history museums in major California banking centers as visible testaments to the impact of the corporation on the state's financial history.[7] Some archival programs, such as that at Control Data Corporation, prepare and distribute departmental histories to new employees, while Chase Manhattan Bank and Weyerhaeuser have initiated oral history programs to supplement their written records and to improve the overall quality of documentation.

The use of archival materials in employee orientation programs, training sessions, company films, and audiovisual presentations underscores the importance of heritage and tradition and helps the work force to develop an appreciation and understanding of the factors that have shaped the business. Successful business archives promote the use of departmental resources as primary training tools and vigorously publicize their availability to communications specialists. Archives such as those at General Mills, Cigna, and The Coca-Cola Company also have developed attractive and educational exhibits that provide still another opportunity to communicate the corporate success stories directly to employees, their families, business guests, and the general public. When Nabisco Brands, Inc. discovered over 1,500 original pieces of advertising art in a company warehouse, their archivist developed an exhibition of the paintings for internal showings and then proceeded to make them available in a traveling exhibit.

A well-managed archival collection will provide perspective on business decisions, allowing companies to understand how they have proceeded from point A to point B. The records will outline the development and implementation of business strategies and will serve to motivate both employees and customers. Executives will make better decisions with a grasp of the institution's development, and employees will gain a better understanding of the company's policies.[8] At the Salt River Project, a public utility, a major archival focus is on issues that historically have impacted the firm's operations. Armed with detailed analytical reports, the office of strategic planning can anticipate problem areas and take corrective action to deal with them.

One of the most tangible and cost-effective justifications for a corporate archival program stems from the protection it affords in matters of litigation. The preservation of the firm's trademarks, slogans, advertising, and promotional concepts often depends on the ability of the archives to document in court a prior, exclusive, or continuous use of the marks. Since the weight of the documentary evidence provided to the court can often be the compelling factor in a judicial decision, the availability of a cohesive body of advertising and marketing documentation has a strong positive impact on the company's legal standing. Similarly, records maintained by the company can yield valuable support data in liability, ingredients, or technical cases that require strong defense strategies. In the legal area alone, the businesses can recoup the total costs of staffing and maintaining an archives. Since the trademarks of the corporation have a value in real dollars, usually expressed as a line item in the firm's annual report, the importance of preserving documentary records forms the first line of defense in many legal proceedings.

From a public relations standpoint, the archives offer myriad opportunities to disseminate corporate messages to widely diverse audiences. The preparation of corporate histories, annual reports, magazines, and other specialized publications often demands accurate and complete historical data, coupled with well-organized visual resources. For example, Gerber, Sears, and Ford have mined archival resources to produce colorful and informative specialized publications to mark anniversary celebrations of note. Additionally, many corporate archivists use the research data they assemble in the course of handling reference requests to prepare historical features for company publications and brochures. The regular exposure achieved in these house organs serves as a continual reminder of the archival presence that can generate even more clients and support. From this same resource base, textbook, newspaper, and magazine writers, together with their colleagues from the electronic media, can develop feature articles and background sketches on aspects of company history and illustrate them with appropriate images. With creative collections management, companies like Corning Glass, with photographic holdings in excess of 150,000 negatives, can fashion positive public relations placements that enhance the public's understanding of the business and its operations.

Successful corporations understand their consumers and respond to their needs. Successful archival programs embrace the same philosophy in establishing their priorities and in marketing their services. Outreach programs can help to stimulate an awareness of corporate products and services in unique ways. At the New York Stock Exchange archivists have conducted lunchtime programs on the history of Wall Street, while Anheuser-Busch, International Harvester, and Walt Disney have developed timely response mechanisms for answering historical or nostalgic inquiries from consumers, and have prepared exhibitions of artifacts and historical documents that have reached consumers in a very personal and direct fashion. As an instrument for informal education, exhibits can both inform and entertain the viewer as they allow the corporation to place its marketing, advertising, and technological achievements in the public spotlight.

Procter and Gamble has gone one step further by producing a series of educational pamphlets designed to supplement social sciences curricula at the junior and senior high school levels. Through the use of photographs, advertising, letters, and documents drawn from the archival collection, these impressive publications position economic history in a very positive fashion while exposing the students to primary source material.

In a few cases, consumer product companies like Sears and Anheuser-Busch can directly influence sales and marketing programs through the

Figure 3. Historical photographs are a key element in most corporate history collections. *Courtesy of The Coca-Cola Company.*

development of packaged goods employing nostalgic themes. Trays, posters, glassware, and memorabilia decorated with designs drawn from archival collections remain staples of the marketing arsenal for sales promotion efforts. Trademark licensing offers still another avenue for revenue accrual, whereby a corporation in return for a royalty allows other manufacturers to use its trademarks and artwork on numerous classes of goods for retail distribution. The availability of strong reference files for licensees enhances the quality of the overall program and directly impacts on the income returned to the corporation.

   While the basic tasks of the archivist to acquire, appraise, process, describe, and reference records do not differ radically from those of associates working in the nonprofit arena, the major functions of any corporate archives are inwardly directed. With few exceptions, the focus of all programming revolves around service to the business and advancement of its goals and objectives. Unlike archival collections at academic institutions, government repositories, and other specialized research centers, outside access to documentation generally is restricted. The archivist serves as the monitor of research activities, balancing the pursuits of the scholar against the company's interest. While corporate archivists strive to open significant segments of their collection for legitimate research topics, many of the records remain closed. In the final analysis, the archivist's loyalty must be to the employer that subsidizes departmental operations.[9]

The types of records preserved in corporations tend to reflect the character of the organization itself. The basics of a good archival collection will include executive correspondence files, minutes of board meetings, records of major committee decisions, and summary financial data, but other elements will vary considerably, directly reflecting business operations. Companies with a strong advertising and marketing orientation generally find their collections weighted in that direction. More audio-visual materials, artifacts, ephemera, product samples, pamphlets, and sales aids of all descriptions find their way into these repositories. Financial institutions, such as insurance companies and banks, face a voluminous assemblage of claims, accounts, and correspondence relating to individual and corporate records, while engineering and high technology firms must consider the preservation of oversized drawings, detailed technical reports, and project files that characterize these businesses. Keeping these unique elements in mind, the archivist strives to develop a collection that represents the totality of the institution.

In most businesses, the archival holdings will represent less than 1 percent of all company records. Consequently, the appraisal criteria used to select this documentation must be based on a clear understanding of the company's history and its information needs. In this one area, historical training has its most immediate and long-term impact. The records classed as historical will determine the shape of future historical analysis of the company and will impose limitations on internal research capabilities. In reaching a decision on preservation, the archivist must always weigh the potential historical value against the cost involved in record keeping and the potential risks inherent with the files themselves. In a litigious age, subpoenas and discovery proceedings can convert a valuable corporate resource into a dangerous adversarial weapon. In some cases the concerns of staff attorneys for certain classes of records can preclude them from archival review, even extending to critical executive-level documents.

A delicate balance exists between the archivist concerned with preservation and the lawyer concerned with potential court action. The more documents that exist in a corporate collection, the higher the risk that materials may ultimately be used by opposing interests. As a result, in many businesses today, records management programs, acting on directives to decrease documentation as rapidly as possible, have assumed the major responsibility for handling the voluminous flow of records. Additionally, telecommunications and computer technologies have further reduced the need for paper records, eliminating even more potential record candidates for archival retention.

In this difficult environment, the corporate archivist must master the fine art of salesmanship and then must meet exacting performance standards in providing needed data in a timely fashion. For the program to succeed, management must recognize the informational value of the

Figure 4. Coca-Cola's history and trademark are used extensively in the company's advertising and marketing. *Courtesy of The Coca-Cola Company.*

assembled collection and must have confidence in the ability of the archivist to balance the needs of research against the interests of the corporation. With management support, the archivist can assemble holdings that represent the corporation in its historical totality. Without that support, the collection's contents will primarily consist of ephemeral items that have little relationship to the decision-making process and the development of the business.

Those factors that are most compelling for retention include age, scarcity, research potential, cost effectiveness, and critical importance. The higher a record scores when evaluated against these criteria, the better are its chances for inclusion in a collection. In many cases the archivist will use sampling techniques in reviewing large record groups such as personnel records or financial reports, while at other times bulky files can be converted to microfilm. The desirable objective is to assemble a collection that is representative and functional.[10]

In 1982 the Society of American Archivists issued a set of guidelines for business archives that were intended to outline a set of "desirable objectives" for companies to meet. Included among them were a written statement of goals and objectives, strong administrative support, independent budgetary administration, adequate space and equipment, and the employment of at least one full-time archivist. The recommendations further suggested that a master's degree in history together with archival experience could qualify candidates to function in a business setting.[11] While doctorates, dual master's degrees, and archival institute certificates often will enhance employment opportunities for candidates seeking academic appointments, corporate employers place much greater weight on the experience factor in making hiring decisions. Most business archivists in administrative positions today had previous work experience in other archival programs. In turn, they tend to hire experienced staff who have already proven their abilities in the archival workplace.

In the most recent survey of business archives conducted by the Business Archives Committee of the Society of American Archivists, 158 businesses reported that they held archives. More significantly, 18 new programs have been established in this decade with projections for a total of 54 new programs in the next few years.[12] Additionally, over 200 representatives of businesses have attended workshops on business archives sponsored by the Society of American Archivists over the last seven years. All of these are encouraging in a period when budgetary constraints are limiting historical programs in many other areas. Still, these optimistic signs must be tempered with the harsh realization that history in the corporate environment must pay its own way. The only utility for history lies in its pragmatic business applications.

NOTES

1. Meyer Fishbein, "Business Archives," *Encyclopedia of Library and Information Science* 3 (New York, 1968), 517–26.
2. David R. Smith, "A Historical Look at Business Archives." *American Archivist* 45

(1982): 273–78. See also Helen L. Davidson, "A Tentative Survey of Business Archives," *American Archivist* 24 (1961): 323–27.

3. Laurence Vail Coleman, *Company Museums* (Washington, D.C.: American Association of Museums, 1943).

4. Robert W. Lovett, "The Status of Business Archives," *American Archivist* 32 (1969): 247–50; Gary P. Saretzky: "North American Business Archives: Results of a Survey," *American Archivist* 40 (1977): 413–20; and *Directory of Business Archives in the United States and Canada* (Chicago: Society of American Archivists, 1980).

5. Margaret Price, "Corporate Historians: A Rare but Growing Breed," *Industry Week* (23 March 1981): 87-90; and Robert Levy, "Inside Industry's Archives," *Dun's Review* (May 1982): 72–76.

6. Betsy Bauer, "Companies Save Past for Future," *USA Today*, 20 March 1984, sec. B, 1–2.

7. For additional discussions of the role of strategic planning in archives, see George David Smith and Laurence E. Steadman, "Present Value of Corporate History," *Harvard Business Review* 59 (November–December 1981): 164–73; and Gilbert Tauber, "Making Corporate History a Planning Resource," *Planning Review* (September 1983): 14–19.

8. James Monteleone, "Your Bank's Archives May be Valuable," *The Bankers Magazine* 166 (January–February 1983): 69–74; and "Companies Digging Up Their Past," *Management Review* 71 (1 January 1982): 32–33.

9. For a fuller discussion of this issue, see Edie Hedlin, "Access: The Company vs. the Scholar," *Georgia Archives* 8 (1979): 1–8; and Anne Van Camp, "Access Policies for Corporate Archives," *American Archivist* 45 (1982): 296–98.

10. For a discussion of appraisal practices, see David L. Lewis, "Appraisal Criteria for Retention and Disposal of Business Records," *American Archivist* 32 (1969): 21–24.

11. Linda Edgerly, "Business Archives Guidelines," *American Archivist* 45 (1982): 267–69.

12. Directory of Business Archives in the United States and Canada (Chicago: Society of American Archivists, 1990). Also unpublished survey data provided to the author by Linda Edgerly, Gary Saretzky, and Karen Benedict, compilers of the data.

Nancy M. Merz, vice president of Archival and Records Management Services for History Associates Incorporated, is a certified records manager. She served as archivist for Texas Instruments Incorporated, planning and directing the establishment of that company's first archives. Merz was formerly regional supervisor for the Local Records Division of the Texas State Library and research archivist for the Colonial Williamsburg Foundation.

STARTING AN ARCHIVES: TEXAS INSTRUMENTS AS A CASE STUDY

Nancy M. Merz

A group of young Texas businessmen recognized a terrific deal when they saw one. Scraping together the necessary cash, they seized an opportunity to purchase an oil exploration company with operations throughout the world. An important segment of the company's work was in the rich oil fields of Southeast Asia. Proudly, they clinched the deal on 6 December 1941. The thunder of bombs and billowing clouds of oily smoke that rose the next morning from Pearl Harbor and elsewhere in the Pacific caused these entrepreneurs to question the timing, if not the wisdom, of their action. Geophysical Service, Inc. (GSI), suddenly seemed like a shaky investment.

But World War II proved to be a boon for American businesses. Stymied by the Japanese occupation of the areas in which it prospected for oil, GSI took its electronic and seismic expertise from the oil fields and brought it into a plant where it began to design and manufacture electronic equipment for the Navy. Soon the electronics business overshadowed oil exploration. By 1951 GSI had become Texas Instruments Incorporated (TI) and within a few years assumed a leadership role in the mass production of germanium and silicon transistors. Later, its engineers invented the integrated circuit and the first electronic hand-held calculator. Texas Instruments bore little resemblance to the small exploration and drilling company purchased in 1941. But because the focus and corporate culture had changed so radically, not everyone remembered the company's previous life.

Texas Instruments first considered establishing a corporate archives in 1980 when Patrick E. Haggerty, TI's youngest founder, unexpectedly died. Although Haggerty's sudden death heightened TI's awareness of the risk to its corporate memory, the company delayed action for several years until the resignation of a long-term board member, who had also served as TI's first corporate secretary and legal counsel. Philip L. Cantelon of History Associates Incorporated, who was then involved with writing a management history for Texas Instruments, questioned the head of the company about the location of the board member's records. Assuming the records were still in his office, the two men rushed down the hall only to find the

Figure 1. The world's first electronic hand-held calculator, invented by Jack S. Kilby, Jerry D. Merryman, and James H. Van Tassel of Texas Instruments in 1967. *Courtesy of Texas Instruments.*

office bare. Later that day, the chairman authorized the establishment of a corporate archives.

Now convinced of the importance of its institutional memory, the company contracted with History Associates Incorporated, a professional archival and historical services firm, to direct the establishment and operation of its corporate archives over a two-year period.

Staffing was one of the earliest concerns of those responsible for the archives project. The average staff of a corporate archives includes three positions: two professional and one clerical. At TI, History Associates provided a supervisory archivist to direct the establishment and operation of the archives and a deputy archivist to assist with that work. TI provided a secretary who, in time, took on more responsibility and assisted with the records work.

A second decision which must be made early on is placement of the project within the larger organization. Ideally the placement should be one that will provide visibility and support, understanding of the goals and functions of an archives, and the necessary financial and administrative resources. Departments which meet this criteria are often those of the corporate secretary, corporate communications, or marketing. The archives at TI became part of the Corporate Communications/Marketing Group, emphasizing its role as an informational resource for management.

A mission statement clearly stating the role of the archives should be written and distributed so personnel of all departments will understand the goals and services of the archives. The History Associates team at TI developed a statement which, after its distribution, became part of corporate policy and procedures, defining and offering examples of appropriate archival records. Also available was a sample list of records which did not have permanent value. Such lists served as illustrations for people unused to thinking about the value of records beyond their immediate purpose.

Soon after the archives started operation, staff also formulated and distributed to researchers procedures for the collection and handling of archival records. Concurrent with organizing records collection, internal policies and procedures for the archives were disseminated and combined in a manual for staff use. Topics included records security, survey, appraisal, processing, transfer, and servicing. An access policy was incorporated into the corporate policy and procedure on archival records.

The greatest challenge facing the team from History Associates was locating TI's archival records among the thousands of cubic feet of materials in storage. The dispersal of records throughout a multinational company and the decentralized organization of that company created additional problems. Over eighty-six thousand cubic feet of records had been stored in a records center operated by the company. Information on records and on past records keeping practices was difficult to obtain because several departments had shared responsibility for records retention: fourteen thousand cubic feet of records were identified as permanent and the remainder destined for destruction after a period of time. Old records had tended to be stored instead of managed.

The History Associates archivists developed a plan to survey systematically material in the records center as well as in active office areas. Believing that the largest number of archival records would be found in the records center, they began that inventory with the permanent material. Concurrently, office surveys started in the older and larger corporate divisions for the same reason.

Because the sheer volume of the records designated as permanent (fourteen thousand cubic feet) prohibited the examination of every box in the records center, the archivists reviewed a computer-generated list of permanent records and selected certain record series for inventory. The contents of some boxes were clearly identified; others were not. Large groups of records, whose contents were not easily discernible from the computer lists, were targeted for sampling.

Anything marked with the name of one of the TI founders, former chairman of the board, or president was inventoried. Boxes labeled with the names of merger partners and acquisitions, significant products and projects, as well as publications and product literature, were examined. In addition, material marked "general" or "miscellaneous" was checked. During the course of the records survey, the archivists found much material with no long-term value in the permanent category, taking up storage space and storage costs over time. An expensive quantity of paper was accumulating additional expenses each year it was ignored.

The archivists read through the nonpermanent list and identified a smaller group of records for later examination. These records were not in danger of destruction because the archives, along with the legal and audit departments, reviewed the annual records destruction list and had the authority to prevent the destruction of any box. Other records noted on the list for destruction were immediately inventoried and some material transferred to the archives. Only a very small percentage of the records planned for destruction were placed on hold and later inventoried. One-fifth of this material was later transferred to the archives.

Simultaneously, records in active office areas were being surveyed by the archivists. The corporate divisions considered most important for the archival survey were the Semiconductor Group, the Defense Systems and Electronics group, and Geophysical Service, Inc. (GSI). The earliest records of the company had remained with GSI, a subsidiary formed in the early 1950s to carry on the original geophysical work of the parent corporation.

Archivists also contacted group managers and asked them to designate a person to help coordinate records survey activities. With this help they were able to compile lists of knowledgeable, long-term employees. These individuals were in turn interviewed regarding records locations and the names of other possible records custodians. Project and product lists also were compiled to aid in the search. In all, over 275 were interviewed. Additionally, the archival team contacted retirees and asked them to donate historically valuable records.

At the end of the second year, approximately eight hundred cubic feet of records had been transferred to the archives. Most of this material was obtained during the second year of operation as a result of records survey activity and heightened awareness of the archives by TI personnel. Nearly 30 percent of the material accessioned during the second year was not solicited but was offered to the archives as a result of in-house publicity; initially, the archivists had arranged for articles in the corporate newsletter as a means of soliciting records.

In all, a little over half of the records came from the TI records center. The rest arrived from active office areas, indicating that many archival records were being maintained by individuals throughout the company. Although emphasis was placed on the records at Dallas headquarters, the archivists later contacted individuals at other sites, soliciting and receiving records from these areas. Archives staff developed a workplan for international records and contacted personnel at foreign sites and subsidiaries concerning archival records.

Processing is usually initiated as material is collected and involves organizing the records, purging routine and duplicate material, describing the contents, and creating finding aids to information. The first large collection processed contained the records of a former president and chairman of the board. When processing was finished, the finding aid was circulated to TI management for comments. The archivists also reviewed processing procedures with management, showing them how boxes of material looked before and after the records were processed. This practice enabled TI management to better understand the amount of work involved with archival processing and the level of information gained. The archivists also explained the cost-effectiveness of processing in terms of retrieval time, quality of information, and volume of material.

By the end of the second year of operation, 41 percent of the material transferred to the archives was fully processed. Smaller groups of records were processed concurrently with large collections, and a balance of administrative and technical material was made available for research. Two archival students from the University of Texas at Austin worked at the archives during the second summer, moving and processing a large collection of records belonging to an early merger partner of TI, the Intercontinental Rubber Company. As a result, this large and mostly forgotten collection, rich in historical material, was made accessible for use.

Education of management to archival policies and procedures is important to the success of any corporate archives. At TI, the archivists held monthly meetings with management, explaining archival policies and procedures, and discussing the goals of the project. For the archives to be successful, visibility and credibility for its services needed to be established. As material was collected and processed, internal publicity was used to encourage research and use of the archives. A column highlighting certain aspects or events in the company's history, based on the material in the archives, was featured in the major newsletter at the Dallas headquarters site.

Modern archival operations include development of a data retrieval system to provide fast and efficient access to information. The archives chose MARCON II for its system because of its global search capability and unlimited fields. Although implementation was somewhat delayed because of the temporary loss of secretarial help, data input and thesaurus development were initiated during the second year.

Use of the archives rose 66 percent during its second year of operation. Researchers tripled and inquiries more than doubled. Primarily, the archives is used by corporate staff to provide information for speeches, presentations, litigation support, public relations purposes, and analyses of past events and programs. It also supplies historical data concerning the company. Material from the archives is in demand not only by headquarters personnel but by researchers from other sites around the country.

Despite a turndown in the semiconductor industry several years ago, the archives was not terminated, a fate which has befallen other company archives. Corporate management realized that it was an integral and cost-effective part of corporate operations. "The nice thing about it is now you can get the facts," said Liston M. Rice, TI's vice president for corporate communications. "Before, we had to base a lot on what people could remember—and you know how wrong that can be sometimes."

Sally L. Merryman was a member of the fourth class in Public Historical Studies at the University of California at Santa Barbara, where she received the master's degree. She conducted water rights research as a consulting historian to Ball, Hunt, Hart, Brown and Baerwitz until 1983 when she joined History Associates Incorporated, working as a research historian and archivist on assignments in Washington, D.C., Tulsa, and Dallas. From 1987 until her death in 1991 she served as the chief archivist/historian for Texas Instruments.

DEVELOPING THE TEXAS INSTRUMENTS ARCHIVES

Sally L. Merryman

In 1984 Texas Instruments Incorporated (TI), a Dallas-based multinational electronics company, contracted with History Associates Incorporated (HAI), a historical and archival consulting firm, to develop an archival program. Early in 1987 TI assumed management of its own archives and began integrating it into daily operations. During the process the archives was able to increase the range of its services to the company while maintaining its high professional standards and regular operations.

In the corporate setting archivists must aggressively seek out every opportunity to expand their sphere of activity to meet their company's needs. This requires both versatility and adaptability on the part of the archives staff, and results in the enhancement of the archives' value to the corporation, thus helping to ensure the survival and growth of the archives during difficult economic times. TI's archival program is one model for developing the role of the archives and increasing its usefulness to a corporation.

THE FIRST NINE MONTHS

During the first nine months of TI management, the archives staff made steady progress in collecting, organizing, and preserving TI's archival records. Records appraisal proceeded on schedule; the level of processing established in 1986 was maintained in 1987; the summer internship program continued; and the backlog of information from the finding aids was entered into the MARCON II computer data retrieval system. With the system 100 percent operational, the staff had the ability to conduct global searches throughout all of the archives' processed holdings. The archives staff also helped evaluate and select a computer system for the company's Media Resource Library.

An earlier version of this article was printed in *PHS Network*, Spring 1990 #20.

Use of the archives was promoted by giving tours to interested founders, board members, corporate officers, individual employees, and groups; providing information about archival records pertinent to various projects; and encouraging site newsletter editors to print articles on the archives. The staff's marketing efforts not only attracted new archives customers, but also resulted in the acquisition of important records.

By the end of the year, use of the archives had increased 63 percent, growing from 177 inquiries in 1986 to 288 in 1987. TI employees used the archival records for research for a variety of projects, including speeches, presentations, analyses of past events and programs, awards nominations, litigation support, and public relations. Moreover, as management became more familiar with the staff's work and its ability to represent TI to the public, an increasing number of outside inquiries were referred to the archives. In 1987, about 12 percent of the inquiries were of this type, whereas only a few such inquiries were handled by the staff in 1986.

Top management, too, began requesting historical information from the archives in 1987, including several volumes of background information for a speech by the chairman of the board on the company's history. The staff's performance in finding relevant documents and providing accurate answers quickly enhanced the perception that the archives was a well-organized, efficient operation and confirmed that the archives contained materials *needed* by the company.

COMBINING ARCHIVES AND PUBLIC HISTORY

The staff had less time available to process records because of their involvement in numerous activities undertaken to commemorate significant anniversaries at TI. The archives received a total of 580 requests for information on the company's history by the end of the year, more than double the number for 1987. Approximately 20 percent of these inquiries came from outside of the company.

The nature and complexity of the inquiries also changed. Ordinarily, the archives received routine requests that could be answered within fifteen minutes. In 1988, however, many inquiries required days or weeks of research to answer.

Some of the lengthier projects included compiling chronologies on various aspects of the company's development; preparing bibliographies; researching information on key engineers and their technical accomplishments for awards nominations; and locating and providing artifacts and documentation for a permanent museum exhibit.

SPECIAL RESEARCH PROJECTS

In 1958, a TI engineer conceived, built, and demonstrated the first semiconductor integrated circuit (IC), an invention that launched a tech-

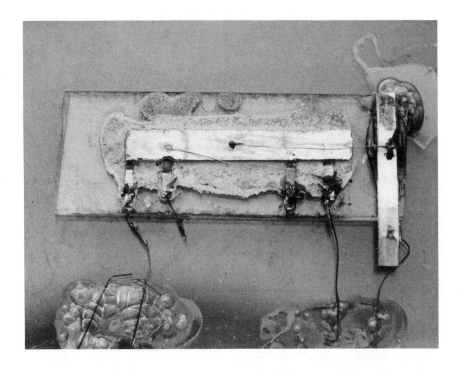

Figure 1. The first integrated circuit (microchip), a phase-shift oscillator, invented by Jack St. Clair Kilby of Texas Instruments in 1958. The integrated circuit was the breakthrough that laid the conceptual and technical foundation for the entire field of modern microelectronics. *Courtesy of Texas Instruments.*

nological revolution. The IC, more commonly known as the microchip, is the foundation of today's multibillion dollar, worldwide electronics industry.

TI's Corporate Market Communications (CMC) department planned to commemorate the thirtieth anniversary of this invention, combining the celebration with a major advertising campaign for the company's current IC products. The theme of the campaign was "Thirty Years at the Heart of Invention." CMC's program centered on obtaining an official Texas Historical Marker, which TI planned to install at its headquarters site and dedicate on 12 September 1988, the anniversary of the demonstration of the first IC. Brochures, newspaper advertisements, posters, and other items also were to be prepared for the campaign.

The archives staff was asked to research and write the history of the IC's invention and demonstration for submission to the Texas Historical Com-

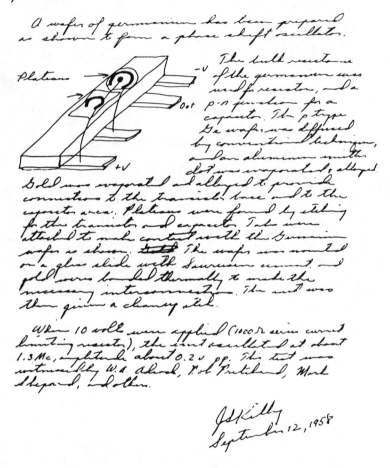

Figure 2. A page from Jack Kilby's laboratory notebook documenting the successful demonstration of the first integrated circuit. *Courtesy of Texas Instruments.*

mission (THC) with TI's marker application. The staff also consulted with market communications personnel during the planning stages of the campaign, provided documentation for materials developed for the campaign, and reviewed various marketing publications for historical accuracy.

Once TI's marker application was approved, the chief archivist served as TI's liaison with the Dallas County Historical Commission and the THC, reviewing drafts of the marker's inscription and helping to keep the process on schedule so that the marker could be installed and dedicated by 12 September. Everything proceeded as planned. The dedication ceremony, which was attended by the Governor of Texas, the IC's inventor, other dignitaries, and hundreds of TI employees, received local, state, and national news coverage.

Shortly after completing the IC history, the chief archivist was assigned the task of preparing a commemorative biography of the chairman of the board, who was retiring from the company after forty years of service. The staff of the archives was responsible for researching, writing, and supervising the publication of the volume, which entailed working with printers, graphic artists, photographers, and bookbinders.

Leather bound copies of the volume were presented to the chairman and his family at his retirement party and one thousand paperback copies were printed for distribution to the board of directors, corporate officers, and managers throughout the company and for use in public relations.

Participation in the historical marker project and preparation of the biography gave the archives much visibility throughout 1988, proved significant in permanently expanding the scope of the archives' services to the company, and afforded the staff the opportunity to develop new working relationships with many people at various levels within TI. During this process, word of the archives spread throughout the company, and staff began receiving numerous inquiries from new archives users in the United States and abroad.

Management also gained a greater appreciation of the role that the archivists can play within TI, with the result that the staff is consulted about the company's history often and continues to receive various research and writing assignments.

Work on exhibits in 1988 led to further expansion of the scope of the archives' responsibilities. Projects included locating and providing artifacts and documentation for a permanent microelectronics exhibit at the Deutsches Museum in Munich, Germany, one of Europe's finest museums of science and technology, and for a display of the company's technical "firsts" at TI's Product Center at Dallas' Infomart. Photographs and artifacts also were provided for a large science exhibit at a local high school.

CORPORATE ARTIFACTS PROGRAM

The Corporate Artifacts Program began in 1984 as an organization separate from the archives to collect artifacts for the Smithsonian Institution. Over time the program evolved into an effort to collect items for TI as well. With the development of the archives' activities in the area of exhibits, management decided in 1988 to place the artifacts program under the administration of the archives. A retired engineer with over thirty-five years of experience at TI was hired to assist in refining and developing the collection.

PHYSICAL FACILITIES

As anticipated during the HAI contract, the archives outgrew its facility by the middle of 1987. Throughout 1987 and 1988 various options to increase storage capacity were evaluated and it was decided that the best long-term solution was to move the archives to a new, larger facility in TI's headquarters building.

In 1988 considerable time and effort went into the planning of the new area. Not only was more storage space required for the archival records, but the staff also needed a larger room in which to process records, an improved room to accommodate researchers, and adequate space to provide for the growth of the archives holdings and its staff.

The area available for the new archives was only about three hundred seventy square feet larger than the area of the old facility. Therefore, to achieve all desired space goals, it was necessary to depart from the use of standard metal shelving and purchase a more expensive, space-efficient, high-density mobile storage system, which doubled storage capacity while allowing for adequate office space and larger processing and research rooms. A sprinkler system was added in the new archives; the stack area was equipped with a motion detector for security and with temperature and humidity controls to provide the best possible environment for the preservation of the records.

RECENT ACTIVITIES

The years following 1988 have been extremely busy for the archives. The relocation to the new facility was accomplished in February 1989, allowing the staff to step up efforts to expand the archives' holdings. Inquiries also increased, with a total of 776 requests for information in 1989 and 1,003 in 1990. Of the 1990 inquiries, about 83 percent were telephone requests, indicating that the archives staff conducted most of the research to answer questions about TI's history.

Work on various exhibits and special projects continued. The staff identified materials for use in a recruitment videotape and a new employee orientation program; located items for use in an exhibit on the history of Dallas businesses; wrote brief histories of various TI subsidiaries; and prepared briefing books for top management on the history of TI's operations in the Asia-Pacific region. In addition, litigation support and the preparation of awards nominations continued. The chief archivist also became more involved in media relations work, hosting television program producers and crews who were preparing documentaries on the history of the semiconductor industry, providing materials for use in these programs, and arranging interviews with key TI inventors. She also prepared a chapter for a report for a major community program headed by TI's chairman of the board and wrote speeches for top management.

DEVELOPING THE IMAGE OF EXCELLENCE

Securing the confidence of management, employees, and outside customers is important to the success of any corporate archives. HAI provided the foundation for this success by establishing sound policies and procedures for TI's Archives, including the organization's commitment to providing prompt, efficient reference service.

Building upon this base, the TI staff refined its customer strategy to meet the company's needs more fully. The archivists are assertive in their marketing of the archives resources and services, staying alert for projects that could make use of the archival records. By keeping current on the archives' holdings, paying careful attention to the informational needs of customers, and researching various aspects of the company's history, the staff constantly improves its skills in guiding researchers to the records most appropriate to their assignments and in answering complex inquiries.

The archivists also are willing to review for accuracy any papers, presentations, speeches, and articles written on TI's history, whether the materials are prepared by TI employees or by individuals from outside the company. Drafts are examined carefully and promptly. The staff's attention to detail in these matters guarantees an accurate end product.

The result of the archives' emphasis on customer service and willingness to assume historical research, writing, and editing responsibilities is that the archives is now viewed by diverse organizations throughout TI as *the* place to go to get the facts about the company's history. Equally as important, the staff is recognized as a team that can be relied upon to produce quality work on time, regardless of whether the work is historical or nonhistorical in nature. These perceptions will ensure the archives' continued participation in a broad range of activities within the company.

FUTURE PLANS

The staff would like to expand its services to TI, but more ambitious long-term plans that promote greater use of the archives will remain on hold until additional resources are available to implement them. Eventually the archivists hope to extend their research and writing services to the preparation of internal reports such as policy or operations histories, litigation research, and the development of fact sheets on frequently researched topics. The reports and fact sheets will reduce the number of in-house papers written on the same subjects, and will be useful to management, the Legal Department, staff speech writers, and media relations, marketing, and advertising personnel. The archivists already have compiled numerous packets of historical information on popular aspects of TI's history to speed responses to customers. In the future, a series of fact sheets on these topics might be developed to answer outside requests for information. TI's media relations personnel would find these materials especially valuable.

Involvement with exhibits is expected to increase as the company's artifacts collection grows. If funding becomes available, the staff hopes to prepare traveling exhibits on TI's history for use at various sites. Moreover, a permanent headquarters exhibit could be developed to educate employees and customers about the company's role in the electronics industry and its contributions to society.

SUMMARY

Versatility and flexibility have been the keys to the development of this organization. Each time the staff of the archives participates in a new project for the company the staff widens its network, opening the way for additional opportunities to be of assistance. The past several years at TI have been extremely challenging, and it has been gratifying to see the many practical and creative ways in which historical information is used throughout the company. The coming years promise to be equally as stimulating as TI learns more about the uses of its history.

Texas Instruments
Access Policy for the Archives

Records are made available in accordance with Texas Instruments regulations and the access policy below. Access to the holdings of the archives is granted under the supervision of the archives staff to ensure the integrity of the collection. Guidelines determining access to specific groups of records are developed jointly by the archives and the department having original custody of the records, in consultation with other appropriate persons when necessary.

Access Policy

Records stored in the archives are categorized and made available in accordance with the following guidelines:

Open Records. Records available to all employees of Texas Instruments. Included in this category are records originally intended for public circulation, such as annual reports, newsletters, press releases, articles, speeches, books, and data sheets. ALL PUBLISHED MATERIALS ARE ALSO AVAILABLE TO THE PUBLIC.

Restricted Records. Records that are open to TI employees at the discretion of the archivist, or in some cases, the Vice President, Corporate Staff.

Closed Records. Records that, for a specified period of time, are available only to the office of origin and the archives staff. Individual exceptions may be made with permission of the office of origin and/or the Vice President, Corporate Staff.

TI personnel who wish to use company records for research unrelated to TI business must receive authorization for the project from their supervisor. (An example of this type of request is a TI employee, working on a degree, who requests the use of the archives for a research paper.) The final product must follow TI's guidelines for safeguarding proprietary information and be reviewed by the researcher's supervisor, and in some cases, the Vice President, Corporate Staff.

Corporate Archives
Mission Statement

The Archives exist to document the evolution of the activities and philosophy of Texas Instruments Incorporated, and to provide an informational resource for TI personnel. The archives staff collects, organizes, preserves, and makes accessible permanent records regarding the company's origin, development, purposes, policies, people, products, and performance. The staff also provides public information on TI's history to researchers from outside the company.

Responsibilities of the archives include:

Developing and maintaining specialized facilities to house the corporation's historical records.

Answering inquiries about the history of the corporation and making historical information available, in the form of original source material, to authorized personnel.

Directing the acquisition and selection of the historical material, giving careful consideration to the informational needs of TI personnel.

Collaborating with other departments to insure the continuous, orderly transfer of historical material to the archives.

Inventorying and organizing historically valuable records for permanent preservation, and developing and administering an information retrieval system for the records in the archives.

Administering procedures for the use of the archives by TI personnel and the public.

Providing pertinent historical information and background material for public relations uses (for books, articles, brochures, advertisements, speeches, television programs, and special events).

Researching and writing histories and supervising the publication of historical reports.

Working on special, nonhistorical projects for management.

Editing and fact-checking documents about TI's history.

Providing artifacts and documentation for exhibits.

Harold P. Anderson is currently vice president and manager of the History Department, Wells Fargo Bank. After receiving his Ph.D. in history from The Ohio State University in 1978, Dr. Anderson was a teaching and research fellow at Stanford University and an archivist at the Hoover Institution. He is a member of the Institute for Historical Study and past chair of the AHA-OAH-SAA Joint Committee on Historians and Archivists.

BANKING ON THE PAST: WELLS FARGO & COMPANY

Harold P. Anderson

How did a miner know that a banker or gold dust buyer was honest, or that he would get credit for the full weight of his gold dust? Through the banker's reputation and use of precision gold standard balances.

In the 19th century Wells Fargo built a strong reputation and used only the best scales—those manufactured by Howard & Davis of Boston (who also made the precision time instruments known as banjo clocks that hung in many offices).

Scene: Wells Fargo Office, Columbus, California, 1859. WF agent has just received scales and reads instructions from San Francisco Office: "It will require great care in unpacking;. . . they are now in perfect order. . . ."

Point: Wells Fargo accounts for your money in the most precise way possible by using the best available technology.

This creative proposal for a television commercial was a moment in history sent in 1985 by Wells Fargo Bank's History Department to McCann Erickson, the bank's advertising agency. A year later it was one of five similar 30-second spots that carried the bulk of Wells Fargo's image advertising in 1986–87.

In a relatively undifferentiated market like financial services, in which most institutions have similar products and services, marketing and advertising are key competitive elements. When a vast majority of an institution's customers are retail, with a strong notion of loyalty to a stable and reliable repository for their money, then history is an important corporate asset.

Wells Fargo has always been conscious of the importance of its history. The stagecoach has been an element of the company's image from the heyday of its transcontinental road life in the 1860s to its present starring role in commercial advertising. In between, the stagecoach rolled through various way stations, mostly in print media, major expositions, and parades, as the notion of "mass advertising" gradually became acceptable to

Reprinted with permission from *The Business History Bulletin* I/1: 9–12.

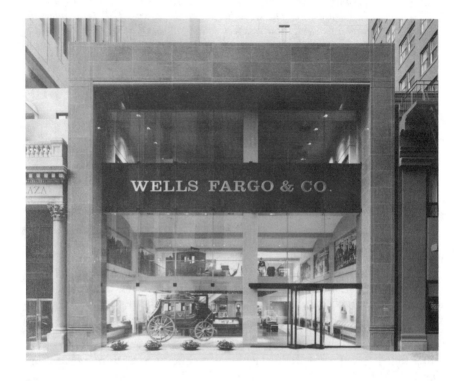

Figure 1. Through boom times and bad, Wells Fargo & Company has become a symbol for the optimistic spirit of the Old West. The stagecoach has been central to the company's image since its creation in the 1860s through its present use in commercial advertising. *Courtesy of Wells Fargo & Company.*

financial institutions in the 20th century. Long after Concord coaches were superseded by other road vehicles, their symbolic value rolled on in the bank's corporate culture and in its presentation of itself to the public. Today Wells Fargo's Concord coach is the most recognized corporate symbol in California.

In the 1930s the bank opened a museum in San Francisco, the Wells Fargo History Room, and in the 1950s instituted a stagecoach program. During the next decade, Wells Fargo commissioned W. Turrentine Jackson, a respected authority on western American history at the University of California, Davis, to investigate the bank's historic right to use the stagecoach symbol and to publish his findings in scholarly journals. When his research led him to the sub-basement of a New York warehouse, Jackson found more than the bank could have hoped for: a virtual treasure trove of Wells Fargo historical records. This discovery together with the approach of the company's 125th anniversary caused Ernest C. Arbuckle, Wells Fargo Chairman of the Board (and former Dean of the Stanford Graduate

School of Business), to set up a task force to study all history-related activities at Wells Fargo. At the end of the study the History Task Force concluded that Wells Fargo's history was a unique corporate asset that needed to be administered with the same care that its financial assets received. It recommended the establishment of a professional program to oversee all history-related activities at the bank; in 1975 the History Department was formed as part of the Public Relations Division.

The new Wells Fargo History Department set forth four simple and straightforward goals that continue to guide them today. They are:

1. To insure the integrity of Wells Fargo's history;
2. To document the origins, development, and impact of Wells Fargo and all of its subsidiaries, affiliates, and merger partners;
3. To provide support to all internal departments of the corporation in their need for historical information and documentation;
4. To serve as a reference center for community groups, scholars, the media, and other corporations seeking accurate information about the history of Wells Fargo and the American West.

Since 1975 the History Department has grown to meet these goals. It currently maintains a staff of fifteen professional historians, archivists, museum and exhibit specialists, and stagecoach drivers loosely organized into three sections: museum group; archives, research, and publications; and the stagecoach program. It has recently been repositioned administratively within the Marketing and Advertising Division.

MUSEUM GROUP

The museum group has expanded far beyond the history room of the 1930s. It now manages museums in Los Angeles and Sacramento as well as in San Francisco with a combined annual attendance of over 100,000 visitors. Each of these museums supports the public relations and business goals of the company through exhibits and programs designed to show Wells Fargo's history in the context of California and western American history. The exhibits emphasize the Gold Rush, the changing nature of banking and the California economy, stagecoaching, and the express business. Historical exhibits of this major component of Wells Fargo's business in the 19th century and early 20th century enhance its impact in the Company's imagery, culture, and business products, viz "Express Banking."

While maintaining similar themes in their exhibits, the three museums have developed individual characters to serve their separate communities. The Wells Fargo History Museum, San Francisco, located in the heart of the city's financial district, was remodeled and integrated with the main entrance to Wells Fargo & Company in 1986. A thirty-three foot glass facade on Montgomery Street provides a warm, western, and inviting passage into Wells Fargo's main banking hall and administrative headquarters. The 6,000 square foot museum displays a variety of colorful exhibits of gold, gold scales, treasure boxes, telegraph equipment, maps, photographs, western paintings, reward posters, guns, Gold Rush era ledgers, western stamps and covers, mining equipment, bills of exchange, a vast array of banking documents, and an original Wells Fargo stagecoach from the 1860s. A series of hands-on exhibits, including a stagecoach under construction, involve visitors in interpreting the story. The exhibit design has been kept clean and simple to focus attention on the artifacts and documents rather than on the architecture.

The San Francisco Museum receives walk-in visitors, gives tours to business and school groups, and hosts receptions for bank-sponsored events with customers. Visitors are addressed with welcome sheets in eight different languages and can purchase mementos at a small general store. The museum is staffed by a curator and assistant curator.

The Wells Fargo History Museum, Los Angeles, is a 5,000 square foot facility, which was opened in 1982. Like many large California businesses, Wells Fargo has its senior managers based in the state's two major metropolitan areas; this museum brought Wells Fargo's history to the Bank's Southern California administrative headquarters. In addition to the exhibits of artifacts and documents, this museum has a small theater for audio-visual presentations and meetings. The curator and assistant curator make over 100 off-site presentations annually on Wells Fargo's history to school, community, and service organization groups.

The third museum, the Wells Fargo Old Sacramento Agency, is on the original site of a Wells Fargo Gold Rush office. It occupies 1,000 square feet in the B.F. Hastings Building, under terms of a lease agreement with the California Department of Parks and Recreation. This museum contains an "Express Stop" automated teller machine in addition to its historical exhibits to serve the large number of tourists visiting Old Sacramento. The facility is open seven days a week and is staffed by a curator and several part-time assistants.

All of the history museums are perceived by Wells Fargo as adding value to its identity, public relations, and macromarketing goals.

ARCHIVES, RESEARCH, AND PUBLICATIONS

The Wells Fargo Archives acts as a core corporate memory to substantiate as accurately as possible "what really happened" and why. One of the facts of corporate life is that people frequently head off in one direction— through transfers, promotions, departures—and the memory and records of what happened on a project head off in another. When I asked Ernie Arbuckle in the late seventies why he established an archives at Wells Fargo (indirectly asking him why I had a job), he said it was simple: he used to attend meetings and listen to people discuss what they *thought* had happened. He wanted a place he could call to get some facts. The Wells Fargo Archives is now such a place.

It contains about 5,000 linear feet of records documenting Wells Fargo's own history as well as the histories of the 300 plus companies (community banks, savings and loans, mortgage companies, express companies, etc.), which have been part of the company's corporate development over the past 135 years. Included in the collections are records ranging in format from Gold Rush era ledgers and documents to modern electronic banking forms. For the years prior to the San Francisco earthquake and fire of 1906 we have what survived in the city and the material discovered by Dr. Jackson in New York. For the 20th century a more rational appraisal process has brought together important corporate records related to decision-making and operations. A project is now underway to establish a computerized data base of the information in the archives.

Special collections of western business records, photographs, oral history materials, and a 4,000 volume reference library on Wells Fargo and related topics complete the information resources of the History Department.

In addition to collecting and organizing historical materials, staff historians and archivists provide a comprehensive research service. Most of the internal requests for information come from the Legal, Marketing, Retail, and Public Relations Divisions of Wells Fargo Bank. It is not uncommon for the staff to produce 5,000 documents for the Legal Division as they prepare a case. Because the stakes are frequently so high in litigation, the archives has proven to be a very valuable property. In the area of marketing, as noted earlier, Wells Fargo relies heavily on historical imagery, provided and verified by the archives. Research for other in-house groups typically involves questions about policy and operations development.

Outside research requests received by Wells Fargo's History Department now approach 1,000 annually. It is our access policy to judge each request on its own merit and try to respond to all inquiries as long as they do not constitute an invasion of privacy or a revelation of a business confidence.

An active publications program is an important part of the History Department's research function. The staff periodically prepares product and market histories, articles for the employee publication, and speeches for senior executives. For external distribution, it produces booklets and pamphlets on the general history of Wells Fargo (such as *Wells Fargo: Historical Highlights*) and underwrites regional and thematic studies by staff members, like Dr. Robert Chandler, and consulting historians, like Dr. Jackson, which appear in western historical journals (in recent years in *Montana History*, *Oregon Historical Quarterly*, *Pacific Northwest Quarterly*, *Idaho Yesterdays*, and *American West*).

STAGECOACH PROGRAM

The final part of the History Department, its stagecoach program, may be the most unusual history-related activity in an American corporation. We manage a fleet of eleven stagecoaches: five original coaches are exhibited in our museums and large offices while one original and five replicas (hand built by Jay Lambert, one of America's last stagecoach builders) are in active use. Each year Wells Fargo coaches appear in about 160 parades, rodeos, civic celebrations, and business promotions throughout California and the West.

Last year over 2.7 million people attended appearances of the stage-coach. These events generated about fifty TV news spots and 100 news-paper articles; popular "historic" occasions translate into new business contacts, reinforce advertising and publicity goals, and create good will.

As I said several years ago in another forum (*The Public Historian*, summer 1981), whether the Wells Fargo experience will encourage others to invest in history is an open question. As our history program has matured, it has been integrated into the business plans and operations of the company. It's managed and judged like a business unit and has added value to the company beyond even the expectations of its original advo-cates. I've even wondered the past few years if it hasn't unconsciously confirmed John Naisbitt's "high tech/high touch" observation in *Mega-trends* that "whenever new technology is introduced into society"—in this case, the electronic restructuring of banking—"there must be a counter-balancing human response." I know that we, as well as our customers, regard our history as humanly comprehensible. I'm not so sure we hail our computers with the same warm regard.

Speculation aside, the key to our success as in any business operation, is having qualified and creative people who know the power of a fact and the value of a dollar.

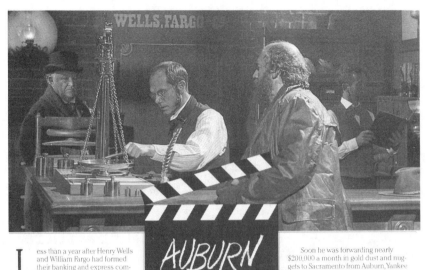

L ess than a year after Henry Wells and William Fargo had formed their banking and express company, young and ambitious John Q. Jackson opened the Wells Fargo office in Auburn, California.

He couldn't have timed it better.

Auburn was an easy ride from Sutter's Mill, where James Marshall had discovered gold four years earlier. By 1852 it had become the Placer County Seat, Crossroads of the Mother Lode. Not bad for a town that started out as Woods Dry Diggings.

Here early stage roads linked dozens of mining camps as a river of gold flowed westward from the foothills toward Sacramento and San Francisco. Today, with Interstate 80 and Highway 49 converging at the town, the Historic Auburn Merchants' Council rightly claims that "All Roads Lead to Auburn."

During the 1850s, Wells Fargo agents like John Q. Jackson worked long, hard hours. Based on letters in the Wells Fargo Archives, this mini-documentary condenses his typical 12- to 14-hour day into 30 brief seconds.

"What I have to do is quite confining — staying in my office all day till 10 at night buying dust, forwarding and receiving packages (and letters) of every kind, from and to everywhere — filling out drafts for the Eastern Mails in all sorts of sums, from $50 to $1,000 and drawing checks on the Offices below, when men wish to take money to the cities, as it is a great convenience to them..."
— Letter from Agent John Q. Jackson to his brother, October 23, 1852

Auburn, California, circa 1857

Soon he was forwarding nearly $200,000 a month in gold dust and nuggets to Sacramento from Auburn, Yankee Jim's, Michigan Bluffs and other offices in his locale.

"At this office from $30,000 to $50,000 and at Rattlesnake Bar office from $30,000 to $40,000 — shipments are made of these amounts once or twice a week centering here. From whence they are sent to the Sacramento office [and] to the San Francisco Mint. When we make a shipment tis frequently 100 to 150 pounds, about as much as one likes to shoulder to and from the stages."
— Letter from John Q. Jackson to his father, September 15, 1854.

O ur cameras caught up with Jackson at dusk, on a rainy night in the foothills. A miner burst through the doors of the Wells Fargo office. "River's runnin' gold," he said in a half-shout, half-whisper. First to one acquaintance, then to another.

Unable to contain himself, he rushed

up to Jackson's counter. "Five ounces, I reckon," he said, as he handed his poke of dust to the agent.

Jackson was as honest and as accurate as his days were long. He prided himself on keeping meticulous records of every ounce of gold dust bought and sold. During the financial panic of 1855, the Company telegraphed that it was desperately short of funds. Jackson paid his depositors, settled his accounts and shipped $15,000 in gold to San Francisco by return express. "The proudest time in my life," he said. That was two days before his twenty-third birthday.

Now Jackson took the buckskin pouch. There was a pause as he weighed the gold on the scales gleaming in the lamplight. The camera cut to the miner's anxious face, then back to Jackson. "Five ounces, *fifteen grains*," he said.

For authenticity, set designers carefully examined numerous 19th century sketches and photographs and built a three-wall Wells Fargo office on a hanger-sized sound stage. They "dressed" Jackson's office with authentic brass scales made by the venerable Boston firm of Howard & Davis and a precision banjo clock also made by Howard & Davis.

Then they duplicated the antique wainscoting and wallpaper. They haunted second-hand shops for a pot-bellied stove, oil lamps, maps and portraits.

How Gold Was Weighed

Gold was (and still is) measured in troy ounces and troy pounds.

1 troy pound = 12 troy ounces of 480 grains each.

1 avoirdupois pound = 16 avoirdupois ounces of 437.5 grains each

1 troy pound = .82286 avoirdupois pound

Note: Agent Jackson's answer to the shotgun in avoirdupois pounds was 96.206. Exactly.

Behind the polished counter of Jackson's desk, they placed ore samples, assaying accoutrements, and the buckskin bags and wax seals for shipping gold dust.

"Auburn" revealed that the Wells Fargo office was not just a bank, express office and stage stop. It was a gathering place for the entire community.

While Jackson took care of banking business, a mother and child waited for the arrival of the coach. An elderly gent read a paper. A customer stood at a counter and rested a dusty boot on the brass rail while he signed his name with a quill pen. A poker game, complete with kibitzers, was in progress at a table near the stove. It would continue until Jackson locked the office for the night. Just out of camera range, the 128-pound bull mastiff that was Jackson's unofficial office mascot watched everything and everyone.

"As a friend, counselor and safeguard, we have one of the largest bulldogs I ever saw in any country. He weighs 128 pounds and is a very intelligent and noble fellow — is devoted to his business and takes as much interest in the office, seemingly, as anyone connnected with the establishment. The first artist that comes along I will have his dogtype taken and forwarded that you may have a look at him."

— Letter from Agent John Q. Jackson to his father, September 13, 1854.

Jackson's reference to "dogtype" was probably a play on the word daguerreotype — a positive photograph made directly on a metal or glass plate. It showed that he had a sense of humor as well as a sense of accuracy. So his answer to the burly shotgun as the stage was about to leave was entirely in character.

"Exactly how much you got in here?" asked the shotgun, wrestling the heavy treasure box into the stage.

"Fourteen hundred and three *ounces*," Jackson replied, using troy ounces instead of the expected avoirdupois pounds.

"Exactly."

Edward L. Galvin is archivist of The Aerospace Corporation, a private nonprofit corporation in El Segundo, California. Prior to joining Aerospace he spent three years as chief of the Local Government Records Bureau at the New York State Archives and Records Administration in Albany, New York, where he directed a program to provide records management and archival advice to over four thousand units of local government across the state. Before moving to New York he was the corporate archivist for MITRE Corporation, a nonprofit systems engineering firm in Bedford, Massachusetts. Galvin holds undergraduate and graduate degrees from Northeastern University in Boston and is a member of the Academy of Certified Archivists.

THE AEROSPACE CORPORATION ARCHIVES: PRESERVING THE COMMON THREAD

Edward L. Galvin

On 20 February 1962, Project Mercury Astronaut John Glenn made three successful orbits of the Earth. Nineteen years later, in April 1981, Space Shuttle Columbia ended its maiden run by gliding to a flawless landing on Rogers dry lake bed in the California desert. The common thread linking these events is The Aerospace Corporation in California. From its early work providing technical direction for the Atlas booster that powered Glenn into flight, to its recent verification of readiness of the Inertial Upper Stage that powered the Galileo Probe into space from the Shuttle Atlantis, Aerospace has been at the forefront of the aerospace industry for thirty years.

Most, if not all, staff at Aerospace will agree that relevant documentation on the company and its technical efforts should be retained and made available to employees who need information on past company activities to aid and assist them with their current work. But coming to an agreement about appropriate organizational arrangements and personnel to serve this function has been a lengthy process. The experience of The Aerospace Corporation can be seen as an example of the problems that classified materials, lack of centralized records storage, and relative youth of the corporation and staff can create for the establishment of a viable archives program. Positioning the archives within the organization, as well as providing its staff access to higher levels of management, can have a dramatic influence on a program and on its priorities for implementation.

There have been some successes in developing an archives program at Aerospace to date. Over fifty meetings have been held with technical and administrative staff members, briefings have been given, nearly two thousand boxes of records in the records center have been reviewed, over 525 feet of archival records have been identified, and more than sixty archival collections have been processed.

How and why Aerospace established an archival program in 1988 can only be understood in the context of the organization's rather complicated brief history. The story of Aerospace begins in the mid-1950s with the development of the Intercontinental Ballistic Missile, the ICBM. At that time, apprehension over the premise of design changes in nuclear warheads led to the creation of the Strategic Missiles Evaluation Committee which recommended a renewed, large-scale effort to develop an ICBM. In 1954, the Western Development Division of the Air Force Research and Development Command was established at Inglewood, California—the first toe in the door in the Los Angeles area.

General contractor responsibility went to the Ramo-Wooldridge Corporation which would later merge with Thompson Products to become Thompson-Ramo-Wooldridge or the more familiar TRW. This was apparently not the best of arrangements, however, as the subcontractors resented Ramo-Wooldridge's "big-brother" role and believed their proprietary business and technological efforts would be infringed upon. To combat this, Ramo-Wooldridge separately incorporated its Guided Missile Research Division as Space Technology Laboratories or STL. STL was barred from any hardware work on the ballistic missile program, but this did little to alleviate the concerns of the other contractors. The Air Force then extended the hardware exclusion to the whole of Ramo-Wooldridge, but this proved to be unacceptable to R-W which proposed a divestiture of STL as a completely separate firm.

Picking up on R-W's recommendation, the Air Force, in March 1960, asked a group of private citizens to organize a nonprofit company. The nonprofit aspect was included in the proposal in order to protect the new company from possible acquisition by holding companies, or even foreign interests, who could control the Board of Directors, thus creating a threat to the development of the Air Force's weapons systems.

First referred to as Corporation "A," The Aerospace Corporation was incorporated in California in June 1960 to succeed STL in supporting military space systems. In 1963 the corporation was designated a "Federal Contract Research Center" (FCRC) indicating its status as a non-academic organization utilizing federal funds for research and development.

Aerospace has participated in most military space programs and in many missile programs over the years, often from the earliest conceptual phases through development, test, and operation. The programs include work with manned and unmanned launch vehicles; satellites for surveillance, communication, and navigation; and ground facilities for satellite readout and control. The company's principal customer is the Space Systems Division of the Air Force Systems Command. Limited support also is provided to other agencies of the federal government.

Today, Aerospace is a firm of over forty-three hundred employees, nearly twenty-seven hundred of whom are members of the organization's technical staff. The company's primary location is in El Segundo, California, in the Greater Los Angeles area, but staff also are located at other sites

Figure 1. The Aerospace Corporation's archives interior. *Courtesy of The Aerospace Corporation.*

across the country. The company's heritage may not be a long one, but it is one of great significance to the U.S. space effort.

Materials may differ, surroundings may be dissimilar, but the activities of inventorying, accessioning, arranging, describing, and providing reference services to records is universal in the archives profession.

Although never formalized as a true archives, Aerospace had the core of an archival program from its earliest days. Company policies and practices included one program entitled "Historical Records." Historical records are defined at Aerospace as "company records for which there is no current need, but which are retained in the records retention center for historical purposes." Although the vague but all-inclusive term of "historical" as used to mean archival records might be misconstrued, the company should be applauded for its early foresight in this direction.

Another company practice entitled "Technical Reports Archives" identifies the central archives for these internal reports as an "important element of corporate memory." Library Services, the archives' parent, is designated as the central company archives for all technical reports. The library has done a superb job of gathering these reports and maintaining one copy of each numbered technical report as an archives collection. Early years of these reports will be turned over to the archives.

There also is a company practice that calls for the library to produce an annual bound volume of reprints of professional papers written by Aerospace staff members. This is referred to as the Professional Papers Archives. One set of bound volumes has already been deposited in the archives.

As for the technical program and project files, provisions have been in place for years for program office staff to cull the important documents from inactive program files, and deposit that material in the records center. These files, if actually extant, will be strong candidates for inclusion in the new archives. Company practices are in place as well for the Records Management Program and the Records Retention program, for the Corporate Executive Files from the General Counsel's Office, and for the Vital Records Program, all of which relate directly to the archives and its work.

With a background such as this, it seems only natural that an archives would be up and running. After all, other similar FCRC's have had archivists on board for many years. However, development of an archives was not to happen at Aerospace until the later 1970s when Aerospace's president commented at a meeting of the Executive Council on the importance of an adequate "corporate memory," noting that it was difficult for the Air Force to maintain such a memory because of the periodic rotation of its key personnel. As an action, the Executive Council directed Administrative Services to review the corporate memory of the program offices.

By 1980 a Corporate Memory Project was in full swing, headed by the Library Director. In her report to the Executive Council in December of that year she mentioned eleven steps to be followed to implement a Corporate Archival Project. These steps suggested designing "a new and ongoing corporate system for capture, organization, and retention of required documentation." The Executive Council in turn directed her to head this expanded effort and chair a task force to implement it.

Subsequently, the president sent a bulletin to all members of the corporation announcing the formation of this new Archives Task Force, citing that

> some of our documentation is fragmented. It consists of individual office, departmental and project records, with no mechanism, even an informal one, tying them together for easy accessibility and reference use.

The goals were to identify data, to provide ready access to information, and to bring uniformity and standardization into the establishment of a true archival system. One member of the technical staff, also a task force member, then prepared an extensive listing of the types of documentation the company would need to retain to document its technical efforts. That listing is still used and continues to be very helpful to the archives program.

By the mid-1980s no archives was yet in place, but a company practice was drafted calling for a "computerized, full-text, data-base system on the company's mainframe, accessible for searches via on-line processing." This proposed system would handle only unclassified records, primarily numbered technical reports. It was not designated to replace original records, only to provide another means of access to the information those records contained. Although there was to be a Central Office of Archives for reviewing all records to be entered into the system, the actual decision making and appraisal authority fell not to the archives office, but to line management.

Finally, the responsibility of setting up an archives was taken on by the new library manager who visited other corporations to determine what she could learn from their experiences. The library joined the Society of American Archivists and the Society of California Archivists and began ordering materials that would be helpful in determining how to proceed.

By August 1987 three official decisions were made: (1) to move the existing records management program from the financial area to Library Services and to eventually combine it with the new archives program, (2) to establish an Archives Advisory Committee, and (3) to hire an archivist.

In October 1988, after a national search, an archivist was hired and charged with establishing a full-scale archival program for the company. The Archives Advisory Committee had been established before the archivist came on board; composed of representatives of the company's three technical groups, the administration group, and the executive offices, the committee meets periodically and is kept posted on recent developments. In turn, members provide the archivist with advice and names of people to contact. Having a committee such as this also helps to lend credibility to the program and provides a cushion of support to a program that could very easily be viewed as a separate adjunct to other company activities.

Action on the third decision, merging the records management and archives functions, will take place at a future date.

IMPLEMENTATION

The Aerospace Corporation's archives is, as stated above, a unit within Library Services. The reporting structure up the line is through the Publications and Briefings Department, and the Administrative Operations Division, to the Administration Group, one of four groups headed by a vice president. Staffed at present by one full-time archivist, the archives has clerical support provided by other offices within Library Services.

The plan which Aerospace formulated for implementing the new archival program may provide some insight on how to proceed in instituting a similar effort in other companies. The following nine points are not necessarily in any order, primarily because many overlap.

1. Know Your Company.

Read and absorb as much as possible about its history. Read annual reports, anniversary books, house organs, technical reports, brochures, and more. This activity should be viewed as part-time and tempered by periods of contact with other human beings.

2. Get Publicity for the Program.

If a program is new, people need to know about it, especially if it is a program that transcends all corridors of the company. If possible, notice should be sent to all employees informing them that an archives has been established or an archivist has been brought on board. The higher the announcement's originating authority the better. An article in the company's house organ can do wonders for the program, but this should wait until there is something worth saying.

3. Identify Records Storage Areas.

At Aerospace it was known that the records center held about fifteen thousand boxes of records, that the library had hundreds of thousands of documents filed on open shelving, and that numerous file rooms were scattered about. In addition, many program offices had held their own records for years. In setting up an archives the company was very vocal about intending to leave the storage situation the way it was. Decentralized storage can be a nightmare for a centralized archival program, but with high security classifications and special access controls such as those faced by Aerospace, decentralization makes sense.

4. Develop Policies.

Two types of policies are needed. One is for the official company policies and practices; the other is for the archives' own internal policies. The former should lay responsibility for the program, define its parameters, and provide access limitations. The latter should explain to depositors and users what they can expect from an archives, e.g., records should not circulate, notes should be taken in pencil, etc. These records are, after all, often one of a kind and care needs to be taken in using them. At Aerospace company policies have been drafted for the archives but have not been instituted pending the uniting of the two records programs.

5. Meet with Records Creators and Inventory Their Holdings.

Meetings with Aerospace staff began with administrative staff rather than with members of the technical staff for several reasons. First, administrative records are more obviously understandable than technical records. Second, administrative records form a solid backdrop for technical program efforts. Accounting records, budget records, and contract documentation all support technical programs and provide layman's insight into records that often are difficult to comprehend. And, third, many technical records at Aerospace and similar companies are government classified. It often takes several months before new employees can have access to any classified documentation. For these reasons it made sense to concentrate on administrative records first.

When meeting with an employee it is ordinarily best to discuss the functions of his office, determine which records he creates or holds, and ask for his opinions on records retention. A follow-up report which includes the archivist's recommendations should be submitted to the employee for concurrence.

6. Design the Necessary Forms.

Cribbing from forms used in other archives is one way to create appropriate forms in rather short order. These forms are necessary for inventorying records, organizing records deposit, and preparing reference requests, and also they can be used as box labels. In dealing with employees used to signature authorizations and detailed records management forms, it is important to lend credibility to the archives by quickly providing reputable looking forms.

7. Process Collections and Create Finding Aids.

Once material is in the archives it should be made available for research purposes. Aerospace staff had been used to depositing records in the records center under their own name, thus ensuring that no one else could have access to the boxes without their knowledge. The records center provides only custodial and retrieval services. An archives assumes responsibility for the records—their processing, preservation, storage, and research use. This distinction is one that must be communicated to donors.

8. Work Towards an Automated Retrieval System.

It is nearly impossible for an archivist to perform his duties in this day and age unless he keeps up-to-date on the latest developments in automated retrieval. Optical disc, CAR, COM, RLIN, MARC are all terms bandied about by those in the records and information fields. More and more users are demanding automated access to collections. After all, several years ago if an archivist had been hired at Aerospace he would have been expected to key-word index every piece of paper in the place. That thinking has blessedly given way, but it is altogether reasonable for users to expect quick and comprehensive service. The way to do that is by automating.

The decision to automate the archives at Aerospace is pending, however, because of renovation of the library building, a major event that eclipsed all others this past year. Completion of the renovation leads to the final element in the company's plan of attack: Space.

9. Find Space for the Archives.

Every archives needs a home, and, like so many others, the Aerospace Archives has been looking for one since the day the program was established. Office space was arranged in the library, but since the plan was for decentralization of storage no provision was made for an archives storage area. Other options considered included shelving space in the library vault or in a similar area in the records center, but no definite decision was reached. The issue became moot, however, in January 1989 when management announced that the twenty-five-year-old library building was to be renovated—gutted wall to wall to meet present building and fire code requirements and also for earthquake reinforcement. Library staff members were relocated to various locations and thousands of boxes of books and reports packed and moved. Archives and the archivist moved to temporary quarters in the records center building.

The enormity of the move is a story in and of itself, but it has turned out to be the best possible circumstance for the developing archives. The necessity of clearing out much of the library vault led to the construction of a new storage vault adjacent to the records center where most, if not all, of the archives will be housed. Since the new vault is not environmentally controlled, it is not a perfect solution, but with some eventual modifications Aerospace could have an archives facility entirely adequate for its needs.

Much remains to be done at Aerospace to get this archival program off the ground and keep it in the air, but the foundation seems secure, the need identified, and the backing in place. Employees at Aerospace are for the most part supportive. They have been gracious and more than willing to give of their time. Understandably there are skeptics, but the company as a whole is planted firmly behind the archival effort.

Numerous program files need to be identified, acquired, and processed. There are laboratory records to deal with, and research and development program files to access. Since archivists usually have a limited scientific, mathematical, and engineering background, there is little chance that the inner workings of all these projects can be easily understood. The answer seems, then, to be to rely on yet another common thread and provide the records creators at Aerospace with guidelines that will help them to identify those records that need to be preserved so that when the time comes to transfer their files to the archives there will be a complete and usable records of the work of which the company is so rightfully proud.

Paula M. Sigman joined the staff of The Walt Disney Archives in 1975 shortly after receiving her master's degree in Library Science from University of California, Los Angeles. For nearly fifteen years she served as assistant archivist of The Walt Disney Company and is now Creative Manager for Disney Character Voices, Inc., a new division of the company established to ensure the integrity and consistency of the Disney characters. She is a member of the Society of American Archivists and the Society of California Archivists, for which she served as president from 1986–87.

PUTTING THE MOUSE TO WORK: MANAGEMENT STRATEGIES AT THE WALT DISNEY ARCHIVES

Paula M. Sigman

Recent professional meetings of corporate archivists have established clear consensus that the time has come for archivists to develop and use recognized management techniques in directing their archives. As we grow in our profession, we have come to realize that the work of the successful archivist can no longer be confined to the materials within his or her care. We must see ourselves as part of a management team, managing not only our collections but also our staff and our departments. And like other members of that team, we must identify and enhance the role we play within our parent institutions.

This is not a simple conceit. In these days of spiraling expenses, corporations and other institutions are looking to cut costs, and they are looking particularly closely at service-oriented, non-profit areas like archives. It is not merely wise, then, but absolutely essential to develop strategies for educating administrators. We need to teach them who we are, what we do, and how we can help them better accomplish their own tasks.

The Walt Disney Archives was established in 1970—fairly late in the life of a company that began in 1923, but over the ensuing decades we have come to be a widely known, integral part of the corporation, and we are securely supported by our top management.

While we have been successful thus far, we do not take that success for granted. Rather we continue to place a high priority on educating management with a number of different ideas and programs. We employ these ideas on a continuing basis to ensure that we maintain management's support. This has become especially important in light of a corporate drama that began a couple of years ago which could have seriously affected, if not abolished, the archives altogether.

Traditionally, The Walt Disney Company has had a high regard for its history. It long has realized the value of its past, and reached into that past to prepare for its future. The Walt Disney Company was among the first of the movie studios to recognize that its films had a life beyond their original release, and it reissues them regularly to delight new generations. Disney films have led to the development of character merchandise—toys, games, clothing, books, records, and other memorabilia featuring the Disney characters. And Disney films have inspired the creation of exciting adventures at our theme parks like Disneyland and Walt Disney World.

When the archives was set up in 1970, it seemed an obvious and natural extension of the company's historical traditions. For the first time materials telling the Disney story were gathered together in a single location, not scattered about in individual departments or even across the country. The staff's knowledge of Disney's history and the collections in the archives makes it easy for researchers, both in-house and from the outside, to obtain the information and answers they need.

The scope of our collection is large, dealing with the history of the entire corporation, not just the Disney Studios. This includes the history of Disneyland, Walt Disney World, Tokyo Disneyland, and other new outdoor entertainment ventures such as the Euro Disneyland project, and the Disney-MGM Studio Tour facility at Walt Disney World. It includes the history of The Disney Channel cable company; Walt Disney Imagineering (which designs our theme parks and attractions) and MAPO (which builds them); the Walt Disney Music Company; Disney Educational Productions—in short, every aspect of the company and product known as "Disney." We also keep the history of Walt Disney and the Disney family.

Serving all these different areas means we have a "constituency" of about thirty thousand people. That doesn't even begin to include the millions of Disney fans worldwide who want to know how much their Mickey Mouse watches are worth, or the game shows which must contact the Disney company to verify the accuracy of their questions and answers, or the students who have questions as they work on dissertations, or the authors who need facts as they write books and magazine articles. The needs of these people, too, are our responsibility. Disney has a special relationship with its fans, or perhaps it is that its fans have a special relationship with Disney. Some of them spend small fortunes collecting Disney art and memorabilia. Adults who grew up with Disney now want to share their childhood experiences with their own children. Part of the work of the archives is ensuring that we have information about the past, and that it remains available for the present and for the future.

At the inception of the Walt Disney Archives, its value seemed obvious. It was supported by a management team that had evolved from the days of Walt Disney himself, people who had grown up with those traditions and attitudes towards Disney's past. Because of that, we did not really need to "teach" them about the importance of the archives. They had affirmed their belief in that value by establishing the department. What we needed to do was develop our identity and then strengthen that identity in our management's eyes.

An excellent way to learn the history of your company or institution is to read anything and everything you can about it. We started with annual

Figure 1. The archives at The Walt Disney Company encourages employees and others to use its facilities. *Courtesy of The Walt Disney Company.*

reports, publications produced by the company to explain its goals and plans to its stockholders. Disney had become a public corporation in 1940, so we had thirty years of documentation, along with thirty years of "hindsight"—knowledge of how those plans had evolved into reality. We read books and articles written on Disney subjects; we watched Disney films and television shows; we visited Disneyland and our other locations with an eye to seeing how the ideas we had been reading about had been realized. We absorbed Disney's history as we went about collecting it.

Once we knew what the archives was and whose history it preserved, it was time to teach others. We enjoyed the endorsement of upper management from the beginning, so our visibility was high. The president sent a memo to every area and every level of the company, announcing the formation of this new division. As we built our collections and defined our services, we discovered the role we could and indeed should play in the company's operation. So we began our task of educating the employees, from top management on down, teaching them what they could expect of the archives.

As our company grew, our responsibilities grew, and so did our opportunities for outreach. We were increasingly secure in our management's support. Then in 1988 The Walt Disney Company underwent a dramatic change in management. Under siege by "business pirates" the company was in danger of being purchased by unfriendly interests who could have split it apart and sold off its assets, piece by piece. (Some of the insider story of this corporate drama is told in a recent book by John Taylor, *Storming the Magic Kingdom*.) To save the company, new management was brought in from the outside, with operating policies and procedures very different from those that had prevailed at the family-founded, family-run Disney studio. To all appearances, it seems that their ideas have worked: we are producing hit films, attendance is up at the theme parks, and we are expanding in new directions and developing major new projects. But this has not been without cost. To help keep expenses down, and profits up, departments and services have been slashed drastically. Some, like our in-house photo lab, and our Studio Library, were eliminated entirely.

The survival not only of the archives, but also of the company's attitude toward its past, depended on the education of management about the importance of Disney's history. In a sense, we had to redefine our identity—to seek out our role in the new goals of the organization and to ensure that we had a place within the new management's master plan. We then had to validate in their view the continued existence of the archives.

The annual report that came out shortly after our new management took charge was invaluable: it outlined for the first time the philosophies and goals of our new team. We supplemented this with magazine and newspaper articles, and with published interviews with key personnel. This may seem obvious, but it is important for the corporate archivist to *read* these materials as well as collect them; they will provide important indication of an organization's development. If the archives does not automatically receive them, ask for copies of speeches by management. Not only does this keep the archives informed, but it assures management that you are interested in what they are doing and that it is worthwhile enough to be preserved in the company's archives.

The most effective way we educate our management is just that: we teach. Because of its strong use of its history, Disney has set up familiarization programs for all employees, at all levels. The archives works closely with our training and development division, called the Disney University, and has become an integral part of that training. Their first day on the job all locally based employees go through a full day of orientation, which includes half-hour presentation in the archives. We give an introduction to the archives and its services, tour the group around the displays, show them how to use our catalogs and finding aids, and then answer questions. At the end, we hand out a brochure which describes our collections in more detail. We invite employees to come back and visit us at their leisure, noting that we stay open through the entire day so that if they have visitors they are welcome to bring them by, even during lunch. Most importantly, we remind them that we are there to help them get the information they may need to do their jobs. The brochure lists our phone number, so it is easy for people to reach us. By giving them this kind of handout, when they leave these new employees carry a bit of the archives with them. They do come back.

This orientation program, "Traditions," takes place every Monday morning. If the group is too large to tour the archives comfortably, we go through the orientation twice. Once a month we present a similar but more in-depth program for management-level employees. There also are special monthly seminars for executive secretaries and administrative assistants, and, when needed, individual presentations for new top executives. We rearrange our regular work around these orientations, and the Disney University has come to value them so much that if we have a conflict they will reschedule to meet our needs.

Prior to each program we receive a list of the participants and the area of the company in which they work. We tailor each orientation to the individual group to highlight their particular needs and the ways in which they can use us. We always focus on what we can do to assist them in their work. The benefits of this kind of program cannot be overemphasized.

This program brings management into the archives, where they can *see* what is done. However, some of Disney's new management were reluctant to take the time to go through such an orientation and kept putting it off. Finally the university scheduled programs for after work and Saturdays and we were able to reach everyone. We have had to be flexible enough to participate in these seminars, and have made it one of our highest priorities.

We also had a lucky opportunity early in the new regime. Our chairman of the board, Michael Eisner, was filming a "lead-in" to "The Disney Sunday Movie" in the lobby of our building, right next to the archives. He needed a place where he could use the phone in between takes. The archives is situated right off the lobby, with an open door leading into our reading room. For four hours Michael popped in and out, and when he wasn't using the phone, he looked at our displays and he asked questions. He also watched us at work. We did not stop what we were doing just because the chairman was there. By the end of the filming he had a pretty good idea of what we do and how we do it.

Not everyone can come into the archives; that is especially true for The Disney Corporation as we have employees stationed all over the world. So we have had to figure out ways to bring the archives to them. The brochure is a start. But here are a few more approaches.

We provide telephone reference and produce special finding aids and fact sheets as needed. These are sent out on archives letterhead. We use a logo that visually communicates "archives," and it has been so successful that when the company opted for a "corporate look" in which the stationery for each division has a similar layout and typeface, the archives was able to retain its distinctive design. The "Supplement to All Pictures Book" was published and distributed by the archives as an in-house tool, and the archives' authorship is prominently displayed. As people throughout the company use these reference aids in their own offices, the archives' presence and assistance are reinforced.

We also make a point of going outside the archives and visiting the other areas of our company. This not only reminds people of the archives and its functions, but it serves to strengthen the idea that we are working *for* them and looking out for their future needs. By letting them know we are interested in what they are doing, they become more interested in us and think of the archives when they need information and when they have something they feel we might need.

On or about the archives' anniversary each year, we publish our own annual report highlighting our activities during the past year, noting important projects, visitors, or researchers and listing some of our most important acquisitions. We circulate this throughout the company, to the department heads and areas we deal with most as well as to top management.

We regularly provide the publishers of our company newsletters with news of significant acquisitions, archives activities (including new exhibits), and historical anecdotes. This type of "From the Archives" news can appear occasionally or it can be a regular column. Interesting anecdotes will not only pique your readers' interest, they may also inspire them to come in and tell you additional stories. In our case these columns and other assistance extend to publications designed for the public. We have a regular column in *The Disney Channel Magazine* and are featured often in Disney books and magazines. We write articles for special Disney projects, including record album liner notes, and make sure the archives is given prominent credit. We frequently serve as a film location for interviews or stories on Disney history and fairly regularly are the subject of radio, television, and newspaper interviews ourselves. Most published articles are routed through management on a regular daily news summary; if one slips by, we send it to the clipping department for circulation. We also offer special presentations on Disney subjects to Disney collector groups and other organizations at the company's request.

In addition, we have encouraged our management to check with us before press releases are sent out. They will even call us at home if an announcement is to be made outside of working hours.

We are also part of the final approval process for scripts dealing with historical subjects. We proofread magazine and book manuscripts for accuracy, both for in-house projects, like Disneyland guidebooks, and for outside publishers. We offer corrections as diplomatically as possible. The archives receives generous acknowledgement in the outside publications, many of which could not and would not be completed without the archives' assistance. Our not inconsiderable Publications Department is particularly appreciative of the archives.

We alert management to special commemorative events, like the fiftieth anniversary of *Snow White and the Seven Dwarfs*, and assist them in developing promotions by providing historical information and photographs and material for exhibits. We are available for radio and television interviews for these special events, even if it means taking a phone call at midnight because the radio show is being broadcast live from a foreign country. Occasionally we have done as many as thirty-six interviews in two days.

Figure 2. Publications and other regular communications help the archives maintain a high profile within the company. *Courtesy of The Walt Disney Company.*

The Walt Disney Archives has been fortunate in its high visibility, both to Disney fans and to our own management. We have had to realize that our responsibility to the company concerns not only our past, but our present and our future as well. If Disney is to be able to glean ideas and information from its history that will be useful in developing new films, new attractions, or new projects, it must have adequate access to all of its history.

We have an extraordinary opportunity to advise, and perhaps even to influence, some of the ways in which that history will be used. But we can only do that if we ourselves are used. The information contained within our files will not be of any use if it is not seen. It is vital that we nurture the strong supportive relationships that we have developed. This is one of our highest priorities.

When new management came in and began re-designing the company's operations, we were obviously concerned. But we applied all of these strategies, beginning with a re-evaluation of our role in the corporate structure. We proffered information, services, and materials that would be useful to management as it formulated new corporate goals.

Have we been successful? Use of the archives has increased; we have doubled our staff, and multiplied our responsibilities, our services, and our budget. We have taken over the responsibilities of the defunct photo lab and turned it into a Photo Library. We are busier than ever. Through educating our management about the use and potential of the archives, we have gained their respect and support. Our value to the company continues to rise, and we are able to fulfill our mandate of collecting, preserving, and making available the legacy of Walt Disney.

PART II
MANAGING THE
CORPORATE MEMORY

MANAGING THE
CORPORATE MEMORY

We have seen in the foregoing section that no two corporate archives are exactly alike. One program may have quite different functions and goals from another and employ different tools. Each responds to varying needs of the parent organization and can be as different from another as the larger organizations they serve are different from each other. Still, there are common problems and needs that most managers responsible for corporate archives will necessarily address. The next section describes several of these.

Corporate archivists will encounter the need for an oral history program sooner or later. Philip L. Cantelon, who has conducted numerous oral history interviews for business and government clients, reminds us of the fragile nature of the historical record that exists only in the minds of individuals. He demonstrates as well how this condition is exacerbated by the nature of the modern corporation, with its high mobility on the part of middle and senior level executives, coupled with a growing tendency to acquisition and merger within the corporate world. Warning us that memories may be fallible and that oral histories are most useful if viewed as a supplement to the written record, Cantelon stresses the necessity of deciding beforehand the goals and purposes of such a program. Selection of subjects and interviewers, equipment and location all flow from this decision. Good professional preparation along with basic listening skills is necessary for the useful oral history interview, as well as proper preparation of the subject. An appendix to this section contains guidelines formulated by the Oral History Association, as well as a statement from the American Historical Association on "Interviewing for Historical Documentation." A sample deed of gift providing the legal release is also included; without this release, use of the interview material can be severely circumscribed.

Anne Van Camp discusses a series of issues which have been the source of considerable misunderstanding between researchers and various levels of corporation management: Who should be allowed to use a corporate archives? Under what conditions? For what purpose? While few archives have traditionally maintained written access policies, with help from the Society of American Archivists more archives are establishing them. Many corporations fear unlimited access in the course of legal proceedings. Professional archivists agree, however, that the best defense against unauthorized, inappropriate, or adversarial use of a company's records is a clear schedule of records retention and retirement as well as a well-enforced policy on access. An example of a written corporate access policy appears with Sally Merryman's article in the preceding section.

The kinds of records created by one company will certainly differ from those of another, just as either may bear more or less resemblance to specialized collections in an academic research library. Those concerned with their care, preservation, and use will find invaluable guidance from the well established procedures for arrangement and description developed by professional archivists over the course of many years. Pennie Pemberton explains the reasoning behind these basic principles and shows how they can be applied to the kinds of records likely to be generated in the course of typical business activities: ledgers, board minutes, sales accounts, and so forth. Pointing out the unique storage requirements of corporate records, she ends this section with several examples of numbering systems that may be used as finding aids for typical business records.

Any organization also must have a plan for protection from fire, flood, or other catastrophe involving its vital records—those without which it could not carry on its regular and necessary functions. Julia N. Eulenberg explains how good archives management includes regular conservation planning for day-to-day deterioration, in addition to protection from unexpected records destruction. Disaster recovery planning, she argues, can readily be built into the classic archival procedures of appraisal, arrangement, and description. Much of the success of such a program will depend on the selection and training of appropriate personnel as well as the clear commitment and understanding of top management. Once these are in place, the archivists' chief task is to assess the likely problems to be encountered—earthquake, flood, fire, for example—as well as physical impediments to retrieval and recovery such as high-rise buildings. Finally, Eulenberg reminds us that a disaster recovery plan must take into account existing arrangements with vendors and insurers and what priority the archives will have vis-à-vis the rest of the organization in the event of an emergency. An outline of salvage techniques for particular kinds of records is included.

Sooner or later, archivists are likely to be engaged in litigation research. Federal legislation relating to hazardous waste sites during the 1980s has created a new concern for companies, one that archivists and research historians are increasingly called upon to address. As consulting archivist Shelley Bookspan makes clear, the stakes in litigation over responsibility for waste disposal are high, and the burden of proof frequently falls to an individual corporation in negotiating its fair share of the possible remediation costs. Without an environmental records management system in place, companies are increasingly vulnerable, dependent not only on their own records which are possibly destroyed or haphazardly stored, but also on those of public agencies and historical archives, virtually inaccessible to the inexperienced researcher. Sharing examples from her wide experience with this problem, Bookspan shows us how creative use of internal records—purchase orders or dump tickets, for example, or accounts payable files—as well as those of such external organizations as maintenance contractors can make a critical difference.

As the American economy becomes more and more an information economy—and an automated one at that—the role of the business archivist becomes increasingly intertwined with technological change. Richard N. Katz and Victoria A. Davis describe both the nature and rapidity of these changes and raise several key questions that managers responsible for corporate archives must address: Who, for example, will decide what material is stored in digital form? What standards will govern the access, security, and integrity of data in those systems? Katz and Davis argue that the archivist, whose relationship with the records manager has traditionally been a source of some tension, must become more fully involved in the management of corporate information systems.

For a biographical sketch of Philip L. Cantelon, see p. vii in this book.

"IF ONLY WE HAD TALKED WITH ___ BEFORE": ORAL HISTORY AND THE CORPORATION

Philip L. Cantelon

The story is a familiar one. A corporate executive dies. Gathering at the funeral, co-workers appreciate the personal loss that death brings, but realize for the first time that the treasure of corporate information upon which they relied is irretrievably gone. "If only we had put ___ on tape. And not only his stories. He knew more about the company's history and why decisions were made than anyone." Corporate managers and fellow workers, who depend on historical experience to help solve current problems, lament the loss of the past. For what has vanished is a crucial source of information, a resource used daily in determining what happened and how it occurred. What cannot be regained is the institutional memory lost.

Some companies don't realize they have a history. At a recent *Inc.*-sponsored conference for the fastest growing private corporations in the United States, one entrepreneur proudly proclaimed that his firm always looked ahead, not back, and therefore had no history. Then he proceeded to tell his audience the corporate success story by narrating the company's history. What he really meant when he said his business had no history was that it didn't have any "old" or historical records in the archival or museum sense of the term. In fact, its history was in his head. Unfortunately, when he moves on, retires, or dies, that wealth of historical information goes with him.

Just as the physician first inquires into his patient's medical history in order to make an accurate diagnosis and informed prognosis, so the business executive must have the very best information available to make intelligent decisions. Part of that essential body of information is the corporate history. The history may be found stored in the company's archival records, stuffed in office file cabinets, or carried in the heads of its employees. Archivists and records managers dig out and protect the first two sources, but oral historians collect and preserve the unwritten record. An oral history program, then, should be viewed as part of an entire effort to preserve and use a fragile and sometimes irreplaceable corporate asset: its history.

The need to preserve personal memories and experience is critical, especially if we subscribe to the notion that experience is a great teacher and that we can draw on lessons from the past. Fewer and fewer corporations have a family-oriented management in which events of today, yesterday, and yesteryear are passed down to each generation, forging a chain between the present and the past. Such a connection enables each manager to assimilate gradually the corporate culture and its historical evolution. Today, instead of this continuum, mid- and senior-level executives drift from corporation to corporation with increasing ease and frequency. Corporation takeover, friendly or hostile, further disrupts connections between management and the corporate culture and corporate history. New managers bring with them financial or marketing or administrative expertise, but they lack the anchor of history in understanding the company's business and its relationship to its customers, its suppliers, its regulators, and itself. To understand and appreciate fully the present nature of a corporation is to know its past. An oral history program can help attain that goal.

This is not to claim more for oral history than it merits. No institution relies solely on the recollections of its "old timers" to debate and determine policy. Paper and electronic records remain the basic reference documents, if they still exist. But oral histories can be a critical supplement to the written record, for the "hows" and the "whys" of decision making are rarely kept on paper. The fact that a particular policy was made and adopted may be clear, yet often the reasons behind its formulation and adoption are obscured by the passage of time or the reasons are just forgotten. Oral history interviews, then, enable a company to fill those gaps in the documentation, to supplement the written record, and to preserve systematically information that might otherwise be lost.

ESTABLISHING AN ORAL HISTORY PROGRAM

The key to any historical resource program is its goals. Goals determine the use and the users. Without a clearly defined need, a program has no users, no constituency, no raison d'être. Therefore, the first step in establishing an oral history project is to determine its goals and purpose. To do this one should ask, "Who in the company will use an oral history project? Why do they need the information? And will the program become a financial liability or will it demonstrate cost savings over time?" Answering these questions lays the groundwork for an oral history project.

Oral history collections exist in a wide range of corporations: banks, pharmaceutical companies, high technology research and development firms, defense industries, communications corporations, construction companies, breweries, law firms, and many more. Usually corporations consider oral histories as more than a deference to the ego of a senior executive, though occasionally this is reason enough to begin a program. In some corporations oral history interviews are used to enrich newsletter articles, respond to stockholder and public inquiries, and enliven advertising campaigns. Some use the information as part of employee orientation programs or as a reference source for managers seeking a historical perspective to a current problem. And others simply wish to build a corpus of information garnered from the experiences of retiring corporate executives, understanding that such knowledge will be as important in the future as it was in the past.

Whatever the situation one inherits, the first goal should be to design an oral history project that has support from top management and a useful purpose within the corporation. Senior executives, public relations and corporate communications departments, marketing programs, the corporate secretary and legal staff, the research and development department, technical and financial divisions—in short, nearly anyone in the organization is a potential client of an oral history program.

DESIGNING AN ORAL HISTORY PROGRAM

Oral history programs can assume a variety of sizes, travel in a number of directions, and take on several levels of sophistication. Crucial to success is to design a program which matches available personnel and financial resources. If either is overtaxed, the quality of the program can suffer. Decide how large a net the program should cast. Starting with a limited number of interviews may be best as one can always expand. An ambitious program that fails to meet its goals runs a substantial risk of being not only cut back, but cut out.

An oral history program should be focused to avoid random interviews. Who is to be interviewed will be shaped, in part, by the goals and purposes of the oral history project. If the goal is to collect blue-collar histories or advances in technology, one will not need to focus much on executives. If the emphasis is on management and corporate policies, a different set of interviewees is required. Oral histories of a department or division or of the development of a particular product may necessitate interviews with people from all levels. Attempts to capture the changes to a corporate culture caused by mergers and/or acquisitions will entail a still different approach. Whatever the focus, however, thorough research combined with assistance from corporate insiders will prove most helpful in establishing an initial interviewee list.

Keep the number of interviews limited in the first year or so and have it approved by top management. It is far easier to add a name than take a person off the list. Most people feel that their role in the company is or was important. They'll ask why they are not on the list. Simply explain that the time and resources available prohibit including everyone who should be interviewed. Resist firmly any attempt to expand the list to include peripheral sources, even though someone believes it may be good politics to do so. Again, time and money prevent it. As ghoulish as it sounds, the oral historian's schedule also is dictated by age and health considerations, as well as by an individual's knowledge and contributions.

How complex or sophisticated a program will be is also determined by financial and personnel considerations. Although a number of programs do not require that the interviews be transcribed, transcription is vital to continued use and information retrieval. Indexing is also a valuable option and worth the additional expense if the collection is used frequently for reference.

One individual within the corporation must be given the responsibility and the authority to make decisions for the Oral History Program. The person should have sufficient standing within the company to assist in explaining the project to potential interviewees at all levels and to arrange interviews. The person may serve as project director with funding control and the ability to hire others to do the actual interviewing. As an alternative, the principal interviewee could serve as the project director operating within an established budget. In any case, it is essential to have full support—conceptual as well as financial—from the very top of the company.

Once a program is underway, oral history exit interviews with individuals who are about to retire or leave the company is a good method for collecting and keeping current information.

The following is a list of possible corporate interviewees:

• founders
• chairman, CEO
• president
• senior vice president
• division directors, department heads
• members of the board of directors
• former executives and directors
• former employees
• long-time current employees
• others outside the company who may have had an effect on its development, *e.g.*, government officials, local politicians

SELECTING AN INTERVIEWER

In defining the users of a collection, one begins to establish the nature of the oral histories. Clearly, to be utilized in a sophisticated manner, the interviews must be sophisticated as well. A collection of humorous anecdotes from the past or a tape recording of a group of "good ole boys" swapping yarns around a table, enjoyable as they may be, will have limited corporate use. On the other hand, a series of professional interviews conducted after thorough research and preparation into the major historical topics, themes, and issues in the corporation's history can provide and preserve perspectives available nowhere else. Over a period of years such histories will become an integral part of the corporation's information resources, a ready reference to the past.

The natural inclination is to choose an interviewer already familiar with the workings of the company. Often this is a recent retiree of long service, who is hired to do the oral histories. From a manager's point of view, this looks like good business practice. It is not necessary to pay for "getting the interviewer up to speed" since the individual "knows where all the bones are buried." Less articulated is the fact that the people in the company can still pick the retiree's brain for his institutional memory.

This approach has its hazards, however. While a long-time employee may know many details of the company's history, he or she also carries the bias and preconceptions of long association. In addition, the person rarely carries the status to be at ease with senior officials or to ask probing questions. Not surprisingly, it is not unusual for a former employee/interviewer to reminisce more during an interview than the person being interviewed.

The best choice is an experienced interviewer who understands that oral history has an equally important aural component. The most competent interviewer is a good listener who has researched the history, has a firm grasp on the topics to be covered, and has the ability to pursue the history in a disinterested way. Moreover, professionally trained oral historians know how to do the background research, which typically involves documentary materials in the company's own records as well as outside institutions. A senior official can be more effectively interviewed by a professional oral historian, who enjoys a certain measure of scholarly prestige, than by an untrained, retired employee. Finally, all information from the interviews, of course, should be considered proprietary by the interviewer until management and those interviewed open the work to the public.

The place to start in locating a professional who may best meet your corporate needs is in the directory of members of the Oral History Association, available from the association's executive secretary. Members are listed alphabetically and by geographical area, but not by skill, experience, or quality. Local college and university history departments, the National Council on Public History at Indiana University-Indianapolis, the American Historical Association, the National Coordinating Committee for the Promotion of History, or the Organization of American Historians may be able to furnish additional information about possible candidates to consider (see Appendix D for addresses).

Contact several potential oral historians, ask about their educational background, experience, products, and costs. Ask how they might design a program. Look for special features which might enhance your efforts or best respond to your needs. Remember, the individual must have a personality that will enable him or her to deal with the entire range of your interviewees. Balance experience, cost, product, and personality in making your selection.

THE INTERVIEW

Preparation

Preparation is the key to a successful interview, for without adequate research one cannot ask intelligent questions or pursue lines of inquiry to the depth necessary for a useful interview. Moreover, executives do not have the time to spend with ill-informed and casual interviewers. This preparation can require hours of digging into issues germane not only to the company but to the individual's role in shaping them. It is often helpful to conduct preliminary interviews to reveal additional insights and information. Preparation also involves constructing a draft outline for conducting an interview, including topics that should be thoroughly covered as well as, perhaps, formulating specific questions.

What happens when few records exist to assist in interview preparation? An interviewer should speak extensively with the company liaison and conduct what one oral historian terms "discovery" interviews. Discovery interviews are informal discussions to learn background information, identify important topics, and develop major themes. These interviews are valuable when they supplement documentation; they are crucial when they must supplant the written record when it does not exist.

The person interviewed also should be properly prepared. The interviewer should fully explain the purpose of the interview and the legal ramifications of an oral history. Providing an opportunity for the subject to think about a range of topics is a good idea. Sending particular questions ahead of time is usually less productive, leading to a rehearsed "story" rather than the spontaneous give and take of an interview. To address questions about ownership, literary rights, or any waivers or restrictions, plan also on sending a legal release form prior to the session.

Recently, issues have been raised regarding interviews which contain possible libelous material or proprietary information. Although this happens only infrequently, a company should be prepared for such an eventuality and address how to handle liability and proprietary information matters in establishing a program. Of course, the problem cannot exist until the interviews are completed. It is not for an oral historian to decide that issue or pass judgment on the content of an interview. In a corporate setting it is best for an attorney to review interviews for such potential problems and act accordingly, rather than destroy the entire interview.

Conducting the Interview

An effective oral history interview is more than "good vibrations" between interviewer and subject. Personality includes the ability to get along with the person being interviewed, the flexibility to change directions during the interview, and the knack of asking open-ended questions. Remember the aural part of oral history; for every speaker there should be a listener. Listen carefully, as if you were hearing the story for the very first time. Taking notes during the interview can help focus attention, get the correct spelling of names, and be a valuable reference when you review the tapes. The interviewee should not be the only one working.

A couple of other suggestions. Begin with general rather than specific questions. Do not correct the individual if he or she makes an error. Corrections indicate that the interviewer may know more about the topic than the interview subject. In addition, a series of corrections may shake the confidence the individual has in his or her memory and thereby spoil or end the session.

EQUIPMENT AND LOCATION

Equipment need not be expensive. While some oral history programs rely on professional quality reel-to-reel recorders similar to those President Richard M. Nixon had installed in the recesses of the White House, most programs opt for a standard cassette recorder using sixty or ninety minute cassette tapes. (Any tape with a longer play time is too fragile.) Lapel microphones are the least obtrusive and can provide the best fidelity and the least interference. Recorders do not have to be expensive, but should not be at the low end of the price range, either. One recorder I have found very suitable, although the transformer for the power supply is very bulky and heavy, is the Sony TCM 5000EV. Costs will vary, but a recorder priced between $200 and $400 with a remote microphone should be adequate and very serviceable over time. The recorder should have the flexibility to run on batteries and a wall plug, but always use the power company's electricity when possible. And do not forget to be familiar with and test your equipment beforehand. Or to turn it on.

The best place to conduct an interview is the location offering the fewest interruptions. Beware the telephone. Another problem is caused by air conditioning in modern offices; the tape always seems to pick up the "white noise" of the fans, making transcription more difficult.

More recently, institutions have turned to video oral histories, which are especially effective in demonstrating the workings of out-dated tools, technical equipment, and work place movements. Video equipment may distract both interviewer and subject, but clearly the technology is becoming more and more common. Cameras are becoming smaller and less obtrusive, and it is likely more organizations will move in this direction in the future.

MAKING EFFECTIVE USE OF ORAL HISTORY INTERVIEWS

Some corporations find themselves with an oral history collection not as the result of a conscious decision, but as an afterthought resulting from an earlier corporate history. Interviews may exist in the form of tape recordings or as collections of file folders containing yellowed pages of handwritten notes. Occasionally, the interviews are transcribed or abstracted. Less frequently are they indexed. Sometimes they are never used again. Not using the information is the same as not having it. Modern corporate historians and archivists are concerned with the availability of information in their collections. If executives involved in organizational planning and decision making do not know about or have ready access to oral history interviews, there will surely come a time when the cost of their maintenance is deemed an unnecessary luxury.

Transcribing

Should oral history tapes be transcribed? The simple answer is yes, if you can afford it. Transcription is a time-consuming process that requires a rough draft of the interview, then an editing by both parties (yes, you may remove all the "uhs" and false starts), and a final revision.

Word-processing equipment has shortened revision time, but the initial transcript still must be painstakingly done. One rule of thumb figures that each hour of oral interview will require eight hours of transcribing time. Of course, this will vary with quality of the recording, the speaking pace of the interviewee, and the ability of the transcriber.

Indexing

There are two types of indexing. The least expensive and least satisfactory is indexing by topics pegged to the tape counter on the recorder. This is only approximate as different recorders count at different speeds. More thorough and more costly is indexing by topic and transcript page. Interviews transcribed in this manner can be used far more easily than the tapes themselves and recent developments in word processing software make indexing an interesting option. Oral history program managers may want to experiment to determine if an index to a key interview is cost effective.

Legal Release Forms

Oral history interviews are the legal property of the interviewer and interviewee. To be certain that no copyright laws are violated when the material is used, corporate oral history programs should have a policy of obtaining oral history deed of gift or release forms from each interviewee. John N. Neuenschwander's *Oral History and the Law*, published by the Oral History Association, is the best work on the subject. It can be ordered from the Association at 1093 Broxton Ave., No. 720, Los Angeles, California, 90024. The following sample release form is reproduced from Dr. Neuenschwander's pamphlet.

Sample Deed of Gift Agreement

I, _____ (name of donor), of _____

(address), City of _____, County of _____,

State of _____, hereby give, convey, and assign to

_____, which is currently in possession of my oral

memoir consisting of _____ to have and to hold the

same absolutely and forever. I understand that _____

will use my oral memoir for such historical and scholarly purposes as they

see fit and that by this conveyance I relinquish:

1)   All legal title and literary property rights which I have or may
     be deemed to have in said work.

2)   All my right, title and interest in copyright which I have or may
     be deemed to have in said work and more particularly the
     exclusive rights of reproduction, distribution, preparation of
     derivative works, public performance and display.

I herein warrant that I have not assigned or in any manner encumbered or
impaired any of the aforementioned rights in my oral memoir.
The only conditions which I place on this unrestricted gift are:

1)

2)

3)

I, _____, (as agent for or as the duly appointed

representative of) _____ accept the oral memoir of

_____ for inclusion in the _____.

Dated _____, 19____.

_____   _____
(Signature)   (Signature)

From John N. Neuenschwander, Ph.D., J.D., *Oral History and the Law*, (Oral
History Association): Denton, Texas, 1985.

HOUSING THE COLLECTION

An oral history collection, both tapes and transcripts, should be located in a corporate archives as part of the general historical documentation of the company. That way access to the historical records is regulated so that the materials are not abused or misused and, where required, confidentiality is maintained. An archives also can assure all parties that the interviews will be adequately protected and preserved. If an archives is not possible, corporate libraries or information centers perform similar functions. Whatever the particular situation, oral histories should be treated as part of the corporation's information resource pool from which information can be promptly and efficiently retrieved.

Oral histories are an investment in the corporate past with continuing payoffs in the present and future. Whether the aim of a program is to collect the neglected part of a company's history or to begin a series of exit interviews in the present, an oral history project can, over time, assure a corporation that its collective wisdom will be safeguarded. Best of all, the corporation's valuable perspective on its past and present will be available to the next generation.

REFERENCES ON ORAL HISTORY

Baum, Willa K. *Oral History for the Local Historical Society.* rev. ed. Nashville: American Association for State and Local History, 1987.

Cutting-Baker, Holly, Amy Kotkin, and Margaret Yocom. *Family Folklore Interviewing Guide and Questionnaire.* Washington, D.C.: U.S. Government Printing Office, 1978.

Davis, Cullom, Kathryn Back, and Kay MacLean. *Oral History: From Tape to Type.* Chicago: American Library Association, 1977.

Epstein, Ellen Robinson, and Rona Mendelsohn. *Record and Remember: Tracing Your Roots Through Oral History.* New York: Sovereign/Simon & Schuster, 1978.

Frisch, Michael. *A Shared Authority: Essays on the Craft and Meaning of Oral and Public History.* Albany: State University of New York Press, 1990.

Gordon, Raymond L. *Interviewing: Strategy, Techniques, and Tactics.* rev. ed. Homewood, Ill.: Dorsey Press, 1975.

Hoopes, James. *Oral History: An Introduction for Students.* Chapel Hill: University of North Carolina Press, 1979.

Key, Betty McKeever. *Maryland Manual of Oral History.* Baltimore: Maryland Historical Society, 1979.

Mehaffy, George, and Thad Sitton. "Oral History: A Strategy that Works." *Social Education* 41 (May 1977): 378–81.

Menninger, Robert. "Some Psychological Factors in Oral History Interviewing." *The Oral History Review* 3 (1975): 68–75.

Mishler, Elliot, G. *Research Interviewing: Context and Narrative.* Cambridge: Harvard University Press, 1986.

Nathan, Harriet. *Critical Choices in Interviewing: Conduct, Use, and Research Role.* Berkeley: Institute of Governmental Studies, 1986.

Rosenthal, Bob. "The Interview and Beyond: Some Methodological Questions for Oral Historians." *The Public Historian* 1 (Spring 1979): 58–67.

Anne Van Camp is currently the archivist at the Hoover Institution at Stanford University. From 1979 to 1989, she was archivist and then manager of Information Services at Chase Manhattan Bank in New York City. Since 1984 she has served on the Business Archive Committee of the International Council on Archives and has also been an active member of the Society of American Archivists' Business Archives Section.

ACCESS POLICIES FOR CORPORATE ARCHIVES

Anne Van Camp

In October 1978 the Society of American Archivists adopted a set of access standards in an attempt to encourage equitable access practices in all archives and manuscript repositories and to alleviate some of the criticism levelled against the archival profession for its discriminatory policies. Unfortunately, business archives have traditionally been regarded by scholars as secretive and unduly restrictive about access to records; and it seems they have lagged behind the profession as a whole in terms of complying with SAA access standards.

At present, very few corporate archives have formal access policies. Most are still maintained strictly for internal use, and access decisions are left to the discretion of the archivist. This situation can lead to innumerable problems, and criticism from outside researchers can often result in one-sided, negative reporting. The archivist is placed in the vulnerable position of trying to discern "good" scholars and journalists from "bad" ones. An even greater problem can come from within the company when an archivist is without guidelines or precedents in deciding whether or not an employee from one department can use records from another department.

Quite often, records are deposited in an archives with the stipulation that they be closed indefinitely, or with the unwritten understanding that the archivist will administer them properly. Apart from the personal liabilities involved, the archivist must consider what happens to those records if the office of origin is reorganized, or if the officer who deposited the records is replaced.

Many business archivists argue that they do not have formal policies because they fear drawing attention to sensitive records in their possession. It is true that most corporations today are made wary about their internal records by the numerous cases of litigation brought against them. Rather than ignoring the issue of access, however, it seems all the more important to have a strong protective access policy.

The adoption of a comprehensive and equitable access policy alleviates many of the problems addressed above. If outside researchers feel they are

From *American Archivist*, Vol. 45, No. 3(1982): 296–98. Reprinted with permission from the Society of American Archivists.

being treated fairly, their results may not be so negative. If the policy can be administered equitably, the archivist is not as vulnerable to the consequences of making a bad judgment and may not have to live in fear of seeing his or her name in the acknowledgements of the latest company exposé. If the policy includes reasonable time limits on restrictions, the records are not in danger of being forgotten or closed forever.

Most, if not all, of the SAA Access Standards can be applied to corporate records. While few companies will view their records with the openness that a public library might, business records are not unlike those of a private citizen. Business archivists can and should strive to make available to all researchers, on an equitable basis, those records that have been designated as unrestricted, and to obtain reasonable time restrictions on those records that should be protected.

To achieve the results desired, an access policy should include the following elements: clear descriptions of restrictions, time limits on restrictions, procedures for determining restrictions, and a statement regarding lines of administrative authority.

Assuming that in many cases there will be more than one category of restriction, the first element, definitions of restrictions, should be stated clearly. The following examples are from the Chase Manhattan Bank's policy:

—*Open records* are those which may be made available to employees as well as persons not affiliated with the company. Included are records originally intended for public circulation and other material approved for public release.

—*Restricted records* are those which, though not open to the public, may be made available to employees for business related purposes.

—*Closed records* are those which, for a specified period of time, are available only to the office of origin and the archives staff.

The second major element to be included in an access policy should be time limits on restrictions. Some companies have set 10 years from the time of creation as the limit of closure, with longer periods if necessary. At Chase, records are normally closed for a maximum of 20 years. Exceptions are as follows:

—Records of the board of directors and the executive committee are closed for 50 years.

—Records of such nature that their disclosure would constitute an invasion of personal privacy or a violation of customer confidentiality, or which might reasonably be expected to prove harmful to Chase, are closed for 75 years.

—Other records may be closed for more than 20 years with the permission of the Archives Council (a review committee whose membership is comprised of senior bank executives including, *ex officio*, the executive for corporate communications, the executive for human resources, the corporate controller, the corporate secretary, and general counsel, as well as the archivist).

The third element of the policy should be clear procedures for determining restrictions. The policy should state when and how restrictions are placed on records (for example: at the time of deposit, the depositing officer, on recommendation from the archivist, will determine the appropriate restrictions).

And finally, the policy should clearly state lines of authority and procedures for obtaining access. Some of the points that should be included are:

—The archivist should be responsible for supervising access to the archives, and the holdings should be used only under the guidance of the archives staff.

—A clause should be included to describe how one can obtain access to restricted or closed records.

—Some indication should be given that records will be made available in accordance with archives regulations.

The actual process of writing a corporate access policy and then having it implemented can be a greater exercise in corporate diplomacy. The people involved in the process have their own ideas as to what this policy should accomplish. For the archivist, the ideal situation is a policy that clearly outlines authority and procedures for governing access to records, a policy that is equitable for all concerned users, and one that protects the archives while at the same time making the company comfortable about the archives. And most of all, the policy should be easy to administer.

The corporation's legal staff, on the other hand, may prefer a far more restrictive policy that may also prove more difficult to interpret. But this is as it should be; a legal staff exists, in large part, to protect a company against lawsuits—which in its view can arise out of virtually any item of information.

If a corporation decides to maintain an archives, it incurs risks. Some records that are preserved might, at some point, prove troublesome, embarrassing, or harmful to the company. But the positive factors involved in an archival program—even in the area of legal affairs—generally far outweigh the negative ones. There are innumerable cases in which records preserved in an archives have saved a company from hostile litigation, and members of the legal staff have in many instances become the primary users of corporate archives. If a company is willing to support the maintenance of its records, the archivist must be responsible for insuring that proper protection is given to the information those records contain.

Pennie Pemberton holds degrees from Australian National University and the University of Liverpool. Currently a consulting historian she has served as group archivist and records manager for Pilkington Brothers plc (UK) and as deputy archives officer for ANU Archive of Business and Labor in Canberra. She is a member of the Australian Society of Archivists, the Society of Archivists (UK), and the Business Archives Council (UK).

ARRANGEMENT AND DESCRIPTION OF BUSINESS ARCHIVES

Pennie Pemberton

The purpose behind the arrangement and description of archives is to let the intending researcher know:

- who created the record (which department and which person of what status within the department)
- why the record was created (for what administrative purpose)
- what form the record has (minute book, file of correspondence, etc.)
- what finding aids exist to it (a data base; a card index; a shelf list; the custodian's good memory and longevity)
- and how it relates to other records (whether there are likely to be more records on the same subject somewhere else in the system)

The user may be an employee of the creating organization looking back to the origin of some company policy, seeking early statistics, original specifications of machinery, or early advertising material to use in a nostalgic public relations campaign. The researcher, might on the other hand, be an academic seeking information on the company's role in major political, social, or economic events; or may be a member of the public seeking information about grandfather who was an employee, or a local historian wanting details about a local branch building or factory.

If the records have been properly arranged and described, the researcher—with comparatively little help—should soon be well on his way to discovering whether the information he seeks is in the collection, and if it is, what authenticity it has.

By authenticity I do not mean absolute truth or falsity, genuineness or forgery, but rather the degree of bias. We all know the cliche about witnesses at the accident—their versions, all "true," will vary with their powers of observation, their vantage point, and their descriptive powers. So too a file of private letters between two equally ranked managers may be

Reprinted with permission from *Managing Business Archives*: Papers from a seminar held on 24 July 1986. Arranged by the Business Archives Special Interest Group of the Australian Society of Archivists, Inc., and the NSW Special Library Section of the Library Association of Australia. Edited by Colleen Pritchard, Australian Society of Archivists, Inc., Canberra 1987.

fuller, and more, or less, objective, than the formal letters which pass through the general office system. The report written by an engineer may have a great degree of unconscious bias if his promotion, salary, or even his job depends on it.

For this reason it is very important to know why the records were created. It is also important to know what other records exist in order to build up a more complete picture of events. And to know how the records were originally kept—were they orderly and methodical—or bordering on the chaotic? Did the writer evidently have all the necessary information at hand? If the archives are well arranged and described, the researcher should be well on the way to knowing these details.

These purposes underlying arrangement and description of archival materials have been gathered together into two basic principles which can be seen over and over again in most of the literature:

- the principle of provenance and
- the principle of original order

The principal of provenance is concerned with who and why:

- who created the records and for what administrative purpose
- what status does the creator, whether an individual or a department, have
- are the records the routine recording of events, sales figures, technical data, manufacturing figures, the payment and receipt of monies and its subsequent accounting—or routine correspondence; or are they involved with the creation and administration of policy, minutes, the interpretation of information and so on.

In establishing the provenance of a group of records it is essential to know about the creating organization. It is circular—the more one knows about the company and its development over time, the easier it becomes to establish where the records fit. And the more one deals with the records, the more one learns about the mechanics of the organization and the possibilities and the shortcomings of the records.

The other principle is original order. There may be a strong temptation to put records concerning the same subject together: to sort and arrange the records according to some grand plan, or to rearrange records which had been kept chronologically in their natural state so that everything to do with a product, a service, a building, or an industrial action is kept together. It may be a grand plan but it has several major dangers.

First, it is often hard enough to put a single book on a shelf in a classified library system. Which of its several themes are the most important, or the most relevant to the users of the library? Records are even worse. Files, especially those on policy matters, grow organically. One thing leads to another, and products come and go. Buildings are used for different purposes—they are built, bought, demolished, rebuilt and sold. Systems are changed; managerial structures rearranged; office technologies come and go.

The paperless office has a long ancestry. The quill pen parchment and chest have given way to steel nibs, paper, copy books, presscopy books, typewriters, carbon paper, kalamazoo binders, ledgers, ledger cards, pigeon holes, filing cabinets, and suspended files—all of these have affected record keeping to a greater or lesser extent. And all of them have affected the relationship between the records. The relationship is important, of significance, and it can easily be lost in the creation of the grand plan.

No one single classification system can possibly cope with all these changes over time. Records which grow by continuous administrative accretion are best left the way they grow. This is the negative reason for the principle of original order. There are also positive reasons.

There are often implicit or explicit finding aids which go with the original order—lists of file titles, manuals of instruction of office routine, card indexes, registers of correspondence—can be pressed into immediate service even if they have to be photocopies because the originals are still in use.

Of course, it may well be that there was no original order. The records may have always been in chaos and the only way to find the archival gold that is believed to be there is to impose some order—but say so—give credit where credit is due. These two principles are the rationale behind arrangement and description and they are the good news. Archivists in general agree with them, though with varying degrees of enthusiasm.

The practicalities of arrangement and description—the nuts and bolts of how to do it—present a more complex picture. There are, it seems an almost infinite variety of ways of arranging and describing, all with their defenders and detractors. There is reason for this, no two collections of records are the same. Archives are, almost by definition, unique, but there are some general points which run through all systems.

First some definitions. The smallest building block of archival description is called the item. An item is, for example, a volume or a file—it is rarely less. In these days of huge accumulations of paper it is rarely possible or desirable to work at the level of the individual sheet of paper. And, records are rarely kept at the level of a sheet of paper.

The next level is that of the series—that is, a body of records related by creation or activity. Some series are immediately obvious—a run of leather-bound minute books from 1886; the similarly bound general ledgers from about the same date; the set of neatly ordered subject files kept by the company secretary from the 1920s; the official run of the company's in-house journal; the set of photograph albums made up in the 1930s to show all the company's properties; the run, the dreaded run, of newspaper cuttings pasted into volumes, year by year. Other series may be less clear. Some may be quite tricky. The apparently straightforward general board minutes also may contain the minutes of the finance committee of the executive committee which later move out into volumes of their own. Similarly, the general ledgers may at first be all encompassing, but particular accounts such as clients accounts, purchase accounts, sales accounts, and the capital accounts may soon go off into their own sets of volumes. The accounts may then go to kalamazoo binders, ledger cards, punch cards, and then vanish onto a data base to reappear as mountains of printout or even microfiche. How many series, sub-series, or related series are there?

The next level is that of the record group—defined for these purposes as the unit within an organization which maintains its own record keeping systems. In a small company, or in the very early days of a big one, there may be only a few record groups or even only one—the company itself—but in any company of any size there are many departments, sections, or even individuals who maintain sets of records which are self contained. If a record group equates with an office or department, as most do, it in turn may be grouped, at various times, into divisions or subsidiaries, depending on how the company itself has been arranged and managed over time. All this should be reflected in the arrangement and description.

Arrangement and description are two different but complementary activities which are sometimes put together under the umbrella term—processing. Very generally, arrangement is more concerned with the physical management of the records, and description with their intellectual management. Everywhere along the way they overlap but we will begin with arrangement.

The first step is to discover what exists and establish some sort of accession register. Starting from scratch one will probably be confronted with elderly filing cabinets, anonymous cartons, brown paper parcels which may or may not contain anything useful (nor be accurately described on the outside), the contents of a walk-in safe in the basement, and rumors of 60 tea chests in storage somewhere which are now your problem.

Learn what you can about each group of records. Work through them systematically if superficially and try to judge the provenance—what sort of records and who created them—what quantity, what sort of condition. As time goes on the transfer of records to the archives should become more orderly.

In the best of all possible worlds, the transfer should be the end product of a carefully thought out records management program and should only come through the archives door accompanied by all the necessary documentation. But that is never how it starts.

When some scheme of priorities has been established, work can begin on the arrangement of a group of records. Unpack, study the records, and put them in original order if possible (to do so take notice of numbering systems, the types and colors of file covers, whether groups of file titles are found together—it may well be that they have been packed and re-packed several times with little care), do any basic housekeeping that is necessary, (straighten the papers, remove rusting pins, check the titles and the dates, number clearly and obviously), list, box and shelve. I will come back to numbering.

This basic exercise should produce the basic finding aid—the shelf list—which also can be used as an inventory for stock taking, and a receipt for records received. Use contemporary titles wherever possible and include any existing contemporary numbering, consider possible series titles and descriptions and take notes on what you learn as you go.

The next step is description. As a general rule both the item and the series title should be kept as short as possible and, where necessary, it should be quite clear that titles have been added or imposed. Series titles should include all those details I mentioned at the beginning—how and why the series was created and what form it takes, and the date range.

- Bound monthly general board minutes 1886–1949
  24 volumes
- General correspondence arranged by subject 1913–1954
  107 files
- General ledgers 1886–1920
  7 volumes (index to accounts in each volume)

Where necessary or desirable a series description can be included covering scope, gaps, and related records, especially if they are finding aids. The series can then be listed together by record group.

The next step is an administrative history or note for the record group. If the record group is a department the note should cover when it was established and why, what work it did—and if the work is not new, who did it before, key personnel (names and titles), changes, and demise. As these administrative notes accumulate so will the administrative history of the company or the organization as a whole.

This knowledge of the company's administrative structure is the best finding aid of all. Almost any research question can then be considered in terms of where in the organization that subject would have been dealt with—that is by which department, and how the information would have been kept, in which series, and so on.

This is not to say that additional finding aids should not be created—those which cut across the system I have just described of a record group description, then series list, and then an item or a shelf list. Additional finding aids of any sort can be most useful and time saving but the keyword is 'additional'.

The archivist may soon find that the queries received fall into a pattern and the expenditure of some concentrated effort on, for example, a card index (or data based index) to an especially useful series would be worthwhile. Other elements of archival material which may merit an index might include biographical details of key personnel, the rise and fall of the company's products, buildings, etc., or a particular form, such as photographs—wherever they may be in the files. It is also often very useful to keep track of research done even if it proves negative. This at least prevents wasteful repetition.

All these finding aids can be tied back to the unit, the file, or the volume which is the basic building block of the whole edifice. Which takes us back to numbering, which is what links arrangement and description and all the additional apparatus together. It is therefore a very important matter and one which needs very careful consideration right from the beginning. Every archival item should be clearly numbered in a way that is unique to the item—to make it quite clear that it is part of an archival collection, but also so that the archival number is not confused with any other.

Numbering systems. The first thing to remember here is that we have in library terms, a closed system. The researcher will, I hope, never browse from shelf to shelf, box to box through a collection. He or she should use the finding aids, discover possible sources, make a request for the material, and have the material issued for use. There is no need therefore to keep all the records from the same source, or even the same series, together in a row of boxes or even on a shelf together.

The records should be stored in terms of their physical characteristics—their size, their environmental needs, and possibly their frequency of use. It is very possible that records from the same series will be boxed and stored together as they will have much the same physical requirements, be the same size and have come to the archives together, but this is not essential. That intellectual control is done through the description. Numbering systems tend towards two types—those where all or part of the number has some 'significance', and those where it is almost random, often a straight location number. Some systems number from the item up and others from the record group down, and others again begin at the series level.

The following are some examples using a hypothetical group of records. Let us say that we are dealing with a relatively straightforward matter, a long run of files—say one hundred—created by the Overseas Sales Department, arranged alphabetically by market.

EXAMPLE 1—NUMBERING FROM THE RECORD GROUP DOWN

First it is necessary to allocate some sort of numbering or mnemonic for the Overseas Sales Department, say OS (as opposed to AS or HM for Australian Sales or Home Market); then a number for the series, say '3' ('1' having been allocated to Departmental Planning Meeting: agendas, minutes, and papers and '2' to Market Managers: annual and six monthly reports).

A shelf (item/file) list could then read:

OS	Overseas Sales Department	
	Correspondence concerning markets, arranged alphabetically by market 1954–1963	
3/1	Bahrain	1954–1959
2	Bahrain	1960–1961
3	Bahrain	1962–1963
4	Burma	1963

| 5 | Canada & North America | 1954 |

The file on 'Canada and North America 1954' would therefore have the number OS3/5.

EXAMPLE 2—NUMBERING BASED ON SERIES

Series 548	**Overseas Sales Department.** **Correspondence concerning markets, arranged alphabetically by market 1954–1963**	
548/1	Bahrain	1954–1959
2	Bahrain	1960–1961
3	Bahrain	1962–1963
4	Burma	1963
5	Canada & North America	1954
6	Canada & North America	1955

The file on 'Canada and North America 1954' would therefore be 548/5.
   In both these examples, some provision would be needed to convert these 'finding numbers' into location codes. It is not practical, especially when space is limited, to hold space for more material from the same department or even the same series. There needs to be a key available to the custodian which converts the 'finding number' to a location:
   e.g., in Example 1

OS3	1–100	Main Repository Stack 5 and 6
	101–156	Main Repository Stack 11
	157–182	New Repository Stack 15

   or, in Example 2

Series 548	1–100	Main Repository Stack 5 and 6
	101–156	Main Repository Stack 11
	157–182	New Repository Stack 15

EXAMPLE 3—NUMBERING BASED ON ITEM

   In this 'system' it is possible to combine the 'finding number' and the 'location'. Items are numbered one after the other as they are accessioned.

| 1–100 | **Overseas Sales Department.** Correspondence files containing markets, arranged alphabetically by market 1954–1963. |

101–281	**Legal Department.**
	Property Files 1935–1970
282–340	**Executive Committee.**
	Correspondence files concerning markets
	arranged alphabetically by market 1960–1963.
689–712	**Overseas Sales Department.**
	Correspondence files concerning markets arranged
	alphabetically by market 1960–1963.

The finding aid would then read:

Overseas Sales Department. Correspondence files concerning markets, arranged alphabetically by market 1954–1972.

| 1–100 | 1954–1963 |
| 689–712 | 1960–1963 |

and a composite shelf list—computer aided, no doubt, could then read:

Overseas Sales Department. Correspondence files concerning markets, arranged alphabetically by market 1954–1972.

Bahrain	1954–1959	Location No.	1
	1960–1961		2
	1962–1963		3
	1964–1965		689
	1966–1967		1000

EXAMPLE 4—NUMBERING BASED ON ACCESSION AND ITEM

A variation on Example 3 is to number each accession of records and then sub-number the items within it. For example, Accession 1 could be all the records brought in by the clearout of the Overseas Sales Department, Accession 2 could be files from the Publicity Department, Accession 3 could be the run of Executive Minutes and so on.

Our sample would then read:

Bahrain	1954–1959	1 / 1
	1960–1961	1 / 2
	1962–1963	1 / 3
	1963–1964	14/ 1
	1965–1966	88/ 1
	1967	82/ 3

Where the records 14/1+ and the records 82/3+ are later deposits/ transfers of similar files from the Overseas Sales Department.

In considering numbering systems the following should be borne in mind:

(1)   Numbering systems should be kept simple.

(2) Multiple numbers especially with slashes (/) and hyphens (-) can be confusing.

(3) Every file and volume should have a unique number—sub-numbering of loose papers within a file means weighing the time it will take against the security and reference benefits.

(4) The nexus between the finding aid number and location should be straightforward.

(5) Even if the system is manual and paper based for the foreseeable future, sometime it may be put 'online' and so should be designed as something that even a machine can cope with.

Published lists which show (often by implication) the workings of a numbering system are few and far between. Most of them, in the nature of the archival world, are published lists of government records. They are, however, well worth studying as the principles underlying them are often transferable directly to the archives of business organizations.

Julia Niebuhr Eulenberg is a consultant and educator, with more than fifteen years of experience in the areas of records and archives management, conservation planning for document collections, and disaster recovery planning for business and archival records. A visiting lecturer at the University of Washington's Graduate School of Library and Information Science and to business, educational, historical, and professional groups in the United States and Canada, Eulenberg has published a number of works on disaster recovery planning and the salvage of water-damaged business records.

DISASTER RECOVERY PLANNING FOR THE CORPORATE ARCHIVES

Julia Niebuhr Eulenberg

A company establishes a corporate archives to bring together and preserve records of enduring value. Many of these records have intrinsic as well as informational value. At least a small percentage of them also will fall into the category of vital records—those records an organization must have in order to stay in business. The corporate archivist must set aside time to write a disaster recovery plan that covers this consolidated corporate asset. Despite the pressures inherent in the early days of planning and establishing the new corporate entity, this step should take place as early as possible. Disaster recovery planning for the corporate archives represents a commitment to fully protect permanently valuable records. Disaster recovery planning is the only guaranteed insurance policy for such records.

In the corporate archives, disaster recovery planning should encompass more than unexpected records destruction. The worst enemy of archival materials is not a sudden disaster, but the day-to-day deterioration of records caused by inappropriate handling procedures, the poor quality of original materials, and a lack of environmental controls. If the corporate archivist has not already considered it, now is the time to add conservation planning and its incumbent activities to the roster of archival tasks.

To be effective, the disaster recovery plan must be written, approved by management, and periodically tested. The completed disaster recovery plan documents the location and condition of particularly vulnerable or significant materials, the training of staff members, the establishment of procedures and guidelines for disaster recovery, and the testing, implementation, and revision of the recovery process.

Archivists frequently find that archival processing is best done in phases. To be sure that important tasks are coordinated, many include progressively refined appraisal, arrangement, and description steps in each phase. The most logical way to achieve conservation and disaster recovery planning is to incorporate them into these same phases of archival processing. How is this done?

During appraisal, the archivist assesses records according to an assigned set of values. Some reckoning of these values determines whether or not the materials are accepted into the archives. Early on, the corporate archivist should add conservation issues to those values. Will the effort to preserve these items outweigh—in time and actual dollars—their other values? If so, the archivist may have to reconsider the records' appraisal status.

Similarly, with disaster recovery planning, the archivist should note the vulnerability and type of records media during appraisal. Here, there is less likelihood that the records will not be retained. Rather, the issue is whether these records will require revisions in the disaster recovery plan. If they do, the archivist should make the appropriate revisions as soon as the records are accessioned.

During the various stages of arrangement and description, the archivist will again carry out conservation tasks. Some are simple: replacing metal paper fasteners with noncorrosive materials; unfolding or flattening folded or rolled documents; mending paper. Others are likely to be more complicated: restoring photographs; creating security or preservation negatives; microfilming deteriorating documents; mending ledgers and other bound volumes. The more complicated the technique, the more likely it cannot be taken care of during the standard processing activities. For such items, the archivist should begin to create a list of materials needing similar work. This permits the archives to coordinate related repair tasks.

Disaster recovery planning also can be incorporated into the arrangement and description stages of processing. Again, the archivist will primarily be looking for ways in which the given items affect the disaster recovery plan. Do these new records include photographs, magnetic media, or items printed on coated paper which will thus be particularly vulnerable to water damage or even to high levels of humidity? Can they be arranged or housed so that they are protected against this kind of potential damage? The archivist should then add their specific location, with records media information, to the disaster recovery plan. Vital records information should be updated once the items are described: shelf list information, finding aids, and other vital records information should be duplicated and stored off-site with other vital records.

This type of systematic integration of conservation and disaster recovery planning into the other activities of systematic processing is what makes conservation and disaster recovery planning work in the archives. If these activities had to be done separately, they would probably not take place. As linked activities, they will get done. It is important to note, nevertheless, that the disaster recovery planning efforts described in this section presuppose an existing plan.

Disaster recovery planning involves several general components. In addition, the archivist must consider a number of elements that are unique to the individual archives. This section will look at these various aspects of disaster recovery planning.

ACTIVITIES

The first step in establishing a disaster recovery plan is to secure written *authorization* from the highest possible level of management. It helps if the authorizing individual also conveys information about the planning process to other staff members. A memo to staff is an appropriate way to do so. This acknowledges that disaster recovery planning is important enough to allocate time and funds to, and enables the corporate archivist to proceed with the steps necessary to carry out disaster recovery planning. Furthermore, if the corporate archives must implement disaster recovery activities at any time during the planning process, it is already empowered to do so.

The corporate archives is in a slightly different position in terms of disaster recovery planning than an organization's records center or than other institutional archives. The corporate archives is very likely to be located within the organization's primary facility or corporate headquarters. Therefore, a disaster that strikes the archives is equally likely to involve other parts of the corporate office and other important records. This has significant implications for disaster recovery planning and recovery operations. Individuals potentially available for help in off-site disasters may very well be busy with their own recovery needs. The corporate archivist must contend with this possibility in developing the plan, writing guidelines, and selecting disaster recovery team members.

As soon as the corporate archives receives authorization, it is ready to begin *development* of the disaster recovery plan. This stage involves a learning process. The corporate archivist must discover what types of records the archives keeps, their value, special information about their potential vulnerability, their condition, their location, and other methods of protection that may already have been secured for them.

The corporate archivist will spend considerable time making telephone and personal contacts during the developmental stage in order to resolve important questions:

- To what extent does the geographic location of the corporate archives increase the potential for disaster? What other aspects of location must be considered in disaster recovery planning? What methods of fire suppression are already in place in the facility? Will physical aspects of the archives create disaster recovery problems?
- To what extent are conservation activities already in place in the archives? What has conservation planning revealed about the condition of the collection? Have especially vulnerable records been identified by location? Which conservation activities are scheduled for these records or items?
- Is anyone currently involved in disaster recovery planning for the overall organization? How does this affect the corporate archives?
- What media does the archives collect? Are vendors already involved with the corporate archives in caring for these records? If not, who provides

the best support in the geographic area in which the corporate archives is located?
- Is vital records protection available through an existing records management program? Can it be extended to vital records listed in the archival collections? If not, how will the corporate archives provide this protection?
- Do records-related vendors already provide support to other parts of the organization? Who are they? What records do they support? What are their contractual responsibilities in the event of a disaster?

Before this stage is finished, the archivist has one further learning experience to complete. The corporate archivist will need to become knowledgeable about disaster recovery planning, disaster recovery techniques, and archives conservation. The discussion below provides a start. Several other monographs offer good information that will be necessary in *developing and carrying out a final plan* (see bibliography). A journal devoted to the security of libraries and archives, *Library and Archival Security*, frequently publishes articles on conservation and disaster recovery planning issues. Articles on these topics are published regularly in archives and records management journals. Even better sources, particularly for machine-readable records, are found in various data processing publications.

Today, most organizations with corporate archives are also likely to have a corporate, or special, library. The corporate archivist should ask the corporate librarian to review professional journals and other serial publications for articles on these topics.

This phase of disaster recovery planning research involves the resolution of questions suggested here and elsewhere specific to the individual archives. Once this process is completed, the archivist is ready to begin *writing guidelines*. A disaster recovery plan is of absolutely no value unless it is in writing. There must be more than one copy of the plan, as well. There should be enough copies to assure that a copy is in each archives unit as well as one in the corporate library, one in the records center, one at the archivist's home, one in the office of the authorizing manager, one in the building maintenance supervisor's office, and one for each disaster recovery team member.

The written guidelines should convey adequate information about the collections. Those involved in salvage operations will need this type of detail to carry out initial triage activities. In other words, the written guidelines must specify the location and condition of particularly vulnerable or significant materials. They must describe these materials by type of media, as well as by informational content and intrinsic value. They must include location charts and conservation records. Some of this information may be too voluminous to include in the disaster recovery plan itself. In this case, the archivist may want to consider including these materials in the vital records protection program. They can then be retrieved in the event of a disaster. Despite this suggestion, the archivist should not separately store parts of the disaster recovery plan if they cannot be retrieved within a few hours following the disaster.

The written plan also should include information about the training of disaster recovery team members and special guidelines for training additional staff if needed during the recovery operation. It should include guidelines for implementing the plan, including procedures for alerting the disaster recovery team, appropriate levels of management, and supporting vendors. These procedures, available early in the process of recovery, will go a long way toward insuring the prompt and total recovery of certain types of records. Finally, the plan should include information about testing and about post-test revisions. This type of information will be useful during the secondary phase of implementation.

Disaster recovery planning also involves *selecting a disaster recovery team.* Disaster recovery team members must be capable of quickly and efficiently responding to an emergency situation. This does not mean they will not get tired or momentarily forget what they are supposed to do. However, written guidelines and good training procedures do mean that these moments will be of short duration.

The disaster recovery team consists of what one author has referred to as internal and external networks. The internal network includes individuals who are already part of the organization's staff. Generally, these are individuals who work with the records as part of their normal job responsibilities. Other members of the internal network will include the facility maintenance crew, secretaries and clerks, the organization's public relations office, and other people in similar positions. Some of these individuals may already be handling similar roles for other parts of the corporate office, if the disaster has not been confined to the archives' area. Coordination between disaster recovery plans and teams will then be necessary and should be noted in the archives' written guidelines.

The external network consists of specialists, such as conservators, photographic processing laboratories, microfilm service bureaus, data processing service bureaus, police and fire departments, possible medical service agencies, utilities companies (gas, electric, water, telephone), the insurance company, possible legal services organizations, warehouses and other storage and drying facilities, cleaning services, transportation organizations, and other groups specific to the individual corporate archives' needs.

As soon as the corporate archives has completed the written guidelines and selected a disaster recovery team, the corporate archivist must then return to management for *approval* of the plan as it now stands. At this stage, management completes its responsibility by endorsing the plan. Approval indicates management support for the remaining steps involved in developing the plan, and for the corporate archives' role in implementing the plan, should a disaster occur. Approval also empowers the disaster recovery team, should they need to enter the building, to begin work in time to save documents, or should they need support in engaging members of their external network.

Training should follow approval as soon as possible. Here, the corporate archivist puts into action for the first time all that was learned during the research and development phase of planning. Disaster recovery team members should walk through a mock-up disaster during their training.

Figure 1. Recovery and cleaning of documents. *Photograph by Ray Copin.*

Since water disasters are the most common and are related to fire recovery operations, training usually focuses on this aspect. While training and testing are similar, they are not the same function. Training must concentrate on instilling in the disaster recovery team the information and skills its members will need in order to carry out their roles in the recovery operation. The purpose of training is to understand why certain tasks must be done. The specifics of how those tasks must be carried out should be left to the discretion of well trained individuals faced with the realities of the moment.

An excellent example of this comes out of an east coast flood several years ago. Water-damaged film needs to be kept wet until it can be cleaned, dried, and reprocessed by a photographic laboratory. When only a small amount of film is water-damaged, the general technique is to place the film in plastic garbage cans or other tubs filled with water and transport it to the laboratory. In this situation, the volume of film and the distance between the disaster site and the laboratory made transporting the film in water-filled tubs impossible. But training had instilled in the driver the importance of keeping the film wet. The solution? The driver stopped every twenty minutes on the drive north, pulled off the turnpike at a service station, opened the back of the truck, and hosed down the film.

The best training conveys what is important and why it must be done, but leaves the actual techniques open so that the team member can be flexible in finding a solution.

Training sessions should concentrate on the regular team members. These individuals will be on the front line during the recovery activities. Their skills must be carefully honed so that they can act immediately and in nearly any situation. At least one training session also should be directed at those individuals who will handle communications (telephone trees, public relations contacts with the media, communications during the early recovery phase when standard communications systems may not be in operation, etc.), as well as those who will assist with facilities cleanup and other non-document-related tasks. Like the driver of the film-laden truck, these individuals should be knowledgeable about what could take place in the event of a disaster and what their possible roles might be.

Some disaster recovery vendors have simply hired individuals through newspaper advertisements. While this may work well in salvaging facilities or equipment, it has had a dire effect on the archives forced to use it. Volunteers from the professional archives and library communities; students in archives, library, or museology programs; and volunteers related to the archives itself will all make better adjunct disaster recovery team members than those who do not understand the importance of provenance, original order, and the need to carefully protect items for which no other copy exists.

The corporate archivist should take care in assembling supplementary disaster recovery team members. This represents a possible area of conflict between the disaster recovery team leader, insurance claims adjustors, and outside recovery vendors. The disaster recovery team leader must use every possible influence—from disaster recovery planning approval and authorization signatures and memos to additional upper management support—to insure adequate protection of archival records during the recovery process.

Training sessions also should be directed toward resolving issues with service bureaus and other members of the external network. If contact with the fire department has not yet been made, this is a good time to do it. When fire departments know that a disaster recovery plan is in existence, they will often attempt to work with the team leader in carrying out the plan. While their main goal is the safety of individuals and the facility, they can sometimes coordinate their strategies with those of the plan. Whether the organization is self-insured or is insured through an underwritten policy, the disaster recovery team leader will want to contact the responsible agents to see what regulations must be followed during the recovery activities.

A decent interval should take place between training and the next disaster recovery planning activity, *testing*. The disaster recovery team leader should give team members time to incorporate the knowledge received during training and to settle back down into their normal routine.

The best time to schedule a disaster recovery planning test is outside of working hours. Disasters have a way of occurring during these hours anyway. A weekend is best, because it gives the disaster recovery team leader a good idea of contact availability, how many team members can be assembled with the first contact effort, and response time. Because the test is supposed to approximate an actual disaster, no prior notification should be given. The disaster recovery team leader should simply set the plan in motion and see what happens.

The test is likely to reveal a great deal about the plan. If the planning effort up to now has been adequate, most of the test outcomes will be positive. Even if the planning effort has been superior, however, the test is apt to reveal some inadequacies. Concepts that work on paper frequently do not work when drivers must wend their way through Saturday afternoon football traffic. Still, the archives is lucky if such a minor disaster actually does coincide with the test. A region-wide disaster will produce similar kinds of stresses on transportation networks. A plan designed to deal with a one-room disaster might not be able to cope with a building-wide or regional disaster.

The disaster recovery team participated in the test to ascertain their own skills and ability to respond to a mock crisis situation. The test also represented an audit of the disaster recovery plan itself. The final activity in disaster recovery planning is *revision*. The actual requirements of this step depend on how well the plan worked during the test. If the disaster recovery team and the corporate archivist have done their homework, this step will be fairly simple. If not, the revisions may effectively require the corporate archivist to go back to the beginning and redo the development activities.

Most revisions are simple. The disaster recovery team fine tunes its responses. The corporate archivist contacts members of the external network and resolves potential problems. The team updates telephone lists and establishes a procedure to assure regular updating in the future. Finally, the disaster recovery team leader schedules a second training session—to go over misunderstandings, to reinforce skills and techniques, and to evaluate the test results.

At this point it is also helpful to purchase a minimal amount of disaster recovery supplies. Accumulating these materials in advance allows the disaster recovery team to begin work immediately in the event of a disaster while additional supplies and equipment are being acquired. Minimal supplies include interleaving materials, plastic-sheeting, folders and records boxes, permanent ink markers, pencils, a large screwdriver, a flashlight and batteries, and toweling. The record containers do not need to be acid-free; these are for the interim storage and transportation of documents. Because standard records center containers come dismantled, they are easier to store with other disaster recovery supplies. After this final step, only one disaster recovery activity remains, and it falls outside of the planning activities: *implementation*. The corporate archivist can hope that preparedness is the amulet necessary to ward off a disaster and the need for implementation. If not, the corporate archives has undertaken these planning activities so that it can implement the disaster recovery plan and begin the work necessary to return the archives to normal.

COMPONENTS

Disaster recovery planning is both a general activity that can be applied to any organization and a unique set of circumstances distinctive to a given corporate archives. The remainder of this section is intended to help the corporate archives address those unique circumstances.

Location plays a significant role in determining the likelihood of certain types of disasters and their projected intensity. Some areas are consistently prone to flooding. A corporate archives located in one of these areas will need to be concerned about potential water damage. Disaster recovery planning in this instance may need to focus on both damage containment measures and appropriate recovery techniques. Other areas are predisposed to earthquake, and again the corporate archives will need to take this into account when constructing the disaster recovery plan. Volcano eruptions and the possibility of local fires represent less probable dangers; but both have occurred in recent years, with more or less limited effect on the archives in the area. The point is that a disaster recovery plan must acknowledge potential regional dangers as well as unexpected sources of disaster.

Figure 2. Remains of library reference section. The most intense area of the fire was in the library reference section. *Photograph by Janice Matsumoto.*

Other location factors which the corporate archivist must consider during the disaster recovery planning process include the archives' physical location within a structure. If it is in a highrise building, how will this affect fire suppression, air circulation, the removal of humidity, and security measures during the recovery process? If the archives is in the basement (an unhappy but frequent location for archival collections), what additional measures must the archivist take to protect records against water damage? Finally, the archivist will need to note the location of specific types of records in preparing retrieval and recovery guidelines for the written disaster recovery plan.

The disaster recovery plan must also consider the combination and types of *records media* kept by the corporate archives. While every corporate archives is likely to have in its collections photographs, machine-readable records, and various types of paper, it is the specific combination that will concern the archivist. This combination will affect the makeup of the external network, specific types of recovery activities, costs, and insurance. The same concerns surround the *intrinsic value* attached to one or more items in the collection. Security during the recovery period may be important for items of significant intrinsic value.

Conservation also may have a bearing on disaster recovery planning. In part, this depends on how well conservation activities have been integrated with other archival responsibilities. Of equal consequence is the susceptibility to future damage of items with existing conservation problems. These items may warrant more protection or special handling during the recovery period and afterwards. The greatest concern will be the development of mold on items that appeared to be all right when they were returned to storage. The archivist should check such items regularly and provide special care during subsequent reference, exhibit, and other outreach activities.

While *vital records protection* is not the only consideration in disaster recovery planning, it plays a significant role. Two techniques regulate the protection of vital records: duplication and dispersal. Both are easily done if the primary value of the records is informational or evidential. If the vital record also has intrinsic or archival value, vital records protection must be handled differently, and usually on site.

The corporate archives itself has two issues to deal with in terms of vital records protection. The first concerns corporate vital records which also may have archival value, such as patent and trademark records. Their archival value has led to their placement in the archives. As a result, the corporate archives has two levels of responsibility for such records: vital records protection and archival management. The second issue concerns the archives' own vital records—the records it must have in order to resume business after the disaster. These include finding aids, shelf lists, the disaster recovery plan itself, donor lists, and other records that the archives will need to continue its operations.

The availability of backup copies of such records allows the archives to resume operations and concentrate on the recovery of archival, rather than operating, records. If the organization already has a vital records protec-

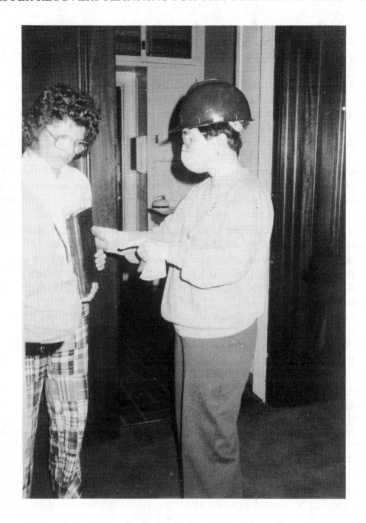

Figure 3. Archivist in fire recovery gear. In her hard hat, mask, leather gloves, identification badge, and rubber boots, archivist Peggy Hansen discusses one of the recovered archival books with Chris Smith Clark, assistant treasurer. *Photograph by Ray Copin.*

tion program, the archives should be able to tie into it. If the organization does not, the archives will need to build vital records protection into its disaster recovery plan.

Two other components relate to the organization's disaster preparedness level: the presence of *a corporate-wide disaster recovery plan* and *insurance*. If the company has a disaster recovery plan that covers the entire organization, the archives' own program will become subordinate to it. This has many potential benefits for the archives: automatic approval, assistance in developing the archival segment of the overall disaster recovery plan, and uniform support and coordination in carrying out disaster recovery activities.

Insurance coverage may be more problematic. In fact, many policies specifically exclude valuable papers from their standard business coverage, so a careful reading of insurance policies is warranted. Valuable Papers coverage is available, but at a fairly high premium. The corporate archivist must be certain that the archives and its contents are included in the organization's policies. In one case, a claims adjustor told a corporate archivist that the archives and its collections would not normally have had any post-fire assistance. Only the insertion of the phrase "and archives" in the policy had assured recovery funds for a major corporate collection.

The requirements for *vendor support services* in disaster recovery planning will vary from one archives to another. Some questions warrant consideration by all archivists. What if this is a regional disaster? Who else will need the services of these same vendors? How will vendors prioritize their clients' needs? The best way for a given corporate archives to find out is to ask in advance—and then to build the negotiated responses into its disaster recovery plan.

Prevention is an early and important step in the disaster recovery planning process. Both water and fire prevention efforts begin with good housekeeping practices. Although fire suppression devices do not prevent fires, they can limit the damage. Even when they contribute to water damage, sprinkler systems can save records. One conservator noted that he always had a better chance of recovering water-damaged documents than he did those burned up in a fire.

Water damage prevention techniques include the use of proper storage areas (basements don't qualify). Suitable detection devices, correctly installed, will alert appropriate personnel to a possible fire or water disaster. A simple containment effort includes having the archives notified when construction or repairs are to take place. Both fire and water disasters have been the result of inadvertent contractor errors. More detailed prevention guidelines can be found in several of the publications listed in the bibliography.

The *type and intensity of the disaster* will determine most of the necessary salvage efforts. These cannot, of course, be predicted in advance. However, the corporate archivist does need to review the disaster recovery plan, disaster recovery team training, and recovery guidelines with various types and degrees of disasters in mind. How will a regional disaster affect the disaster recovery team's ability to respond? Will all of the disaster recovery team be needed in the event of a single sprinkler-head leak? Can the collection remain accessible to users during a simple type of cleanup operation?

In a fire, no one is allowed on-site until personal safety can be assured. What types of activity can disaster recovery team members carry out during this interval, so that they are ready for immediate action when the area is cleared for entry?

Because of the nature of today's buildings, the corporate archivist should not forget chemical contamination as a potential type of disaster. In such cases, access to records may be blocked for some time, even though they are physically intact. However, the most likely disaster is water, because it is at once a damage source of its own and the component of so many other disasters. Corporate archivists will do well to prepare for this disaster as completely as possible, and to be adequately prepared for the others.

The final component of disaster recovery planning is guaranteeing the success of the *salvage* effort. Salvage activities depend on a variety of factors: the records kept, the type and extent of the disaster, the availability of in-house personnel, and the types of insurance coverage, among others. Much of this the archivist will already have addressed during the disaster recovery planning process. But it can be useful to find out who is likely to be conducting the salvage operation for the archives. The insurance

Figure 4. Archival area of library, thirty hours after the fire. Temporary lights are in place in the archival area of the library. Archivist Peggy Hansen points to the book collection still remaining on the shelves. Remains of the rest of the collection are in the debris on the floor. *Photograph by Walter J. Hansen.*

Recovery Priority by Type of Records Media

Media	Recovery Priority	Salvage Techniques				Comments
		Initial		Follow-up		
		Action	Purpose	Action	Purpose	
Magnetic Media Mag tapes Disc packs Floppy diskettes and disks Flexible disks Audio and video tape cassettes	Immediately	Contact vendor. Some success has been obtained in cleaning the surface of water-damaged floppy disks with distilled water. Such action should only be taken under the supervision of a vendor.	To obtain professional advice	May include freeze or vacuum drying, special cleaning techniques or professional assistance in retrieving data.	To remove all moisture and other contaminants from the media; to access data in case of damaged media	Such advice should be sought well in advance of a disaster. Heat and water damage to media may result in subsequent damage to hardware or to irretrievability of data. Proper backup and salvage procedures are essential. It is worth noting that such records are among the easiest to duplicate and store off site.
Photographic Materials Color films and photographs	Immediately	Once wet, keep wet.	To avoid further damage and image loss			Color dyes are inherently unstable and should be handled immediately to prevent loss of color and other damage.

Material	Priority	Action	Reason	Further action	Reason	Notes
Silver or emulsion films and photographs	Immediately	Immerse totally in water.	To avoid further damage			
	Within 48 hrs.	Obtain professional advice and/or assistance with cleaning, drying, and restoring.		Seek professional advice and help with cleaning and drying. Freeze only if necessary.	To restore film to original state. Freezing may lead to image damage, but less damage is likely to be caused by freezing than by delayed treatment.	
				Freeze if professional help must be delayed longer than 48 hrs.	To stabilize color dyes	
Diazo or vesicular (duplicate) microfilm	Last	If time and staff are available, rinse off and lay out flat to dry; otherwise, leave until last.	To prevent water spotting and curling of rolls of fiche	Wash with liquid detergent and rinse and lay out on absorbent paper to dry.	To remove water spots and other contaminants and to restore film	Diazo and vesicular films are nearly impervious to water damage and should clean up easily.

Recovery Priority by Type of Records Media (continued)

Media	Recovery Priority	Salvage Techniques				Comments
		Initial		Follow-up		
		Action	Purpose	Action	Purpose	
Diazo or vesicular (duplicate) microfilm (continued)						Some diazo film produced during the 1970s has a tendency to break down in water, leading to image loss. Diazo films sometimes fade with age. Fading or other damage discovered after the disaster can be related to poor quality control rather than to the disaster.

Paper Bond, rag, duplicating, other	Within 48 hrs. (depending on temperature and humidity levels at disaster site and on extent of damage). In fires, paper is least vulnerable media.	Air dry in well-ventilated area. Interleaving may be used to speed drying. If volume of wet records is large, consider freeze or vacuum drying.	To prevent further deterioration of paper materals and eruption of mold or fungus	May include freeze or vacuum drying. If mold erupts, treat with fungicides. Fumigation can often be combined with the vacuum-drying process.	To remove moisture from materials and to reduce humidity levels in damaged materials; to eradicate mold	In high-humidity levels, deterioration of wet paper records can begin within 2–3 hours.
Coated or clay papers	Immediately	Freeze	To hold damaged materials until freeze or vacuum drying can be arranged	Freeze or vacuum drying	To remove all moisture from paper, without damaging or removing coated surface	Freeze or vacuum drying is the only successful recovery technique for this medium.

Reprinted with permission of G. K. Hall & Co., Boston, from *Taking Control of Your Office Records*, copyright 1983.

company will indicate whom they would contact. The corporate archives should follow up this information with a phone call to find out this organization's experience with archival collections. Few organizations do have experience in salvaging archival collections.

Archives represent an unusual type of salvage effort. The records gathered here cannot be easily replaced, if they can be replaced at all. Their value can be damaged by mishandling as well as by physical loss. Indeed, documents belonging to one record group, but buried in another through careless handling in a disaster may be effectively lost.

In contacting the salvage company, the archivist is following a pattern already set by contacts with vendors, pre-disaster purchases of recovery supplies, and the effort of writing and testing a disaster recovery plan.

The goal is a successful recovery. The technique is footwork in advance. In the event of a disaster, it will have been well worth the corporate archivist's effort to have considered the state of archives in good times and bad and to have developed guidelines for pulling it through the worst of times.

BIBLIOGRAPHY

Banks, Paul. *A Selective Bibliography on the Conservation of Research Library Materials.* Chicago: Newberry Library, 1981.

Barton, John, and Johanna G. Wellheiser, eds. *An Ounce of Prevention: A Handbook on Disaster Contingency Planning for Archives, Libraries, and Record Centres.* Toronto: Toronto Area Archivists Group Education Foundation, 1985.

Bohem, Hilda. *Disaster Prevention and Disaster Preparedness.* Berkeley: University of California, 1978.

Bulgawicz, Susan L., and Charles E. Nolan. *Disaster Prevention and Recovery: A Planned Approach.* Prairie Village, Kans.: ARMA International, 1988.

Cunha, George Martin, and Dorothy Grant. *Library and Archives Conservation: 1980s and Beyond,* v. I and II. Metuchen, N.J.: Scarecrow Press, 1983.

Eulenberg, Julia Niebuhr. *Handbook for the Recovery of Water-Damaged Business Records.* Prairie Village, Kans.: ARMA International, 1986.

Geller, S. B. *Care and Handling of Computer Magnetic Storage Media.* U.S. Department of Commerce, 1983.

Kyle, Hedi. *Library Materials Preservation Manual.* Bronxville, N.Y.: Nicholas T. Smith, 1984.

Protecting Federal Records Centers and Archives from Fire. General Services Administration, USGPO, 1976.

Shelley Bookspan is president of PHR Environmental Consultants, Inc. She holds a master's degree in City Planning from the University of Pennsylvania and a Ph.D. in American history with emphasis in Public Historical Studies from the University of California, Santa Barbara. The author of several articles on the subject of history and toxic waste liability, Dr. Bookspan is a contributing editor of the Real Estate Law Journal *and writes a quarterly essay on environmental topics for real estate law practitioners and other real estate professionals.*

CORPORATE RECORDS AND ENVIRONMENTAL LIABILITY IN THE ERA OF SUPERFUND

Shelley Bookspan

The value of creating and maintaining a usable corporate archives has increased substantially in light of recent federal environmental legislation. In the Comprehensive Environmental Response, Compensation and Liability Act (known as CERCLA, and even better known as Superfund), passed in 1980,[1] and underscored in the Superfund Amendments and Reauthorization Act of 1986 (known as SARA)[2], Congress imposed strict liability on parties named as contributors to a hazardous waste site, regardless of the time elapsed since the dumping, leakage, or "release" actually occurred. Thus, each Potentially Responsible Party (PRP) that the Environmental Protection Agency (EPA), CERCLA's enforcement agency, identifies as contributing to the contamination must pay a proportionate amount of the remediation costs. This is true regardless of whether the waste disposal was legal when done, whether there was any intention to cause harm, or whether many years have since passed.

Only companies with their internal records organized and accessible can respond convincingly once they become PRPs, and yet the stakes are high. At major landfill sites, where numerous industries and municipalities have dumped their wastes legally over the course of decades, but where inadequate protections have resulted in serious soil and groundwater contamination, remediation costs alone can run many millions of dollars. What's more, the legal costs of apportioning strict liability among many defendants can run high as well. Named PRPs, however, have good reason to cooperate in the apportionment process. While even strict liability can prove expensive for a PRP, in a series of cases courts have concluded that CERCLA's strict liability clause does not preclude the imposition of joint and several responsibility.[3] This means that, theoretically, any single PRP can be made to cover the entire cost of a remedial action, if necessary. It also means that the EPA, in the interests of expedience, can stop at naming the PRPs, and let the parties themselves agree on the allocations.

In an attempt to demonstrate whether and how much of the contamination is really theirs, PRPs may take their cases to court. Using EPA estimates of the quantity and types of their wastes, these defendants, usually corporate entities, may present testimony of a variety of scientific experts, such as hydrographers and toxicologists, as well as computer models showing the fate of the chemical wastes at the site over time. Sorting through different views of these complicated issues then becomes the task of the judge and jury. These lay people often believe that they have inadequate understanding or information by which to assess the actual synergistic effects of combined chemicals, the migration of chemical compounds over time, the local hydrogeological conditions, or the biodegradation versus persistence of chemicals in given environments, and, therefore, they believe they cannot allocate responsibility fairly. Some such cases can take months and even then may not come to resolution.[4]

USING CORPORATE INFORMATION

For PRPs with existing corporate assets, it may be preferable to cooperate with the EPA and with each other in negotiating a fair allocation of responsibility. Section 122 of SARA, for example, allows the EPA to initiate a negotiation process. At that time, the EPA sends a notification letter to each of the PRPs it has identified to date. The letter lists all of the PRPs, ranking them according to the volume of wastes each apparently contributed to the site in question, and it also lists the quantity and type of each known waste, by PRP. Each PRP may then respond during the sixty-day moratorium, during which time no additional remediation expenses accrue.[5]

For any given corporation, many dollars can hinge on the outcome of these responsibility allocation negotiations. Unless the corporation has prepared for the eventuality of becoming a PRP by creating an on-line environmental records management system, however, the key to successful negotiations may well lie in a body of corporate files, long inactive and relegated to storage, or even, to a lesser extent, the forgotten files of public agencies and historical archives. These records, produced in an earlier regulatory milieu, may seem inaccessible to a corporation's management information systems staff because they are filed according to defunct or seemingly irrelevant classifications. In fact, sixty days may not be enough to render these files useful at all.

Forward-looking companies that have been in place for many years have come to understand that their chance of becoming a PRP on a local landfill site is great. Generally, the EPA uses a landfill operator's records to identify the PRPs, but such records themselves will be limited for sites operating prior to the late 1970s, when federal laws changed to require more precise accounting by landfill operators.[6] A corporation active in a given community for decades can count on being named as a presumptive PRP at a longstanding landfill requiring remediation. The best way for a corporation to defend against undue liability, however, is to be able to demonstrate actual quantities and types of wastes produced over time and their disposal techniques, as well as to demonstrate the accuracy of the records. In other words, obscure corporate records systematically organized can reveal the missing chapters of the company's environmental history that corporate negotiators will need to reconstruct.

One southwestern utility, for example, recently made just such effective use of its corporate archives. After the EPA named the company as a PRP at a landfill site, this utility was able to produce convincing records demonstrating that it could not have contributed the volumes of a certain solvent waste attributed to it. By filing and properly coding purchase orders for chemicals over a period of decades, the utility was able to show that it did not, in fact, ever even use the solvent found to be contaminating the landfill.

Another successful use of corporate records occurred in regard to a landfill site in a western state where the EPA had identified nearly two hundred waste contributors or PRPs. Several of the largest of the named PRPs were able to produce precise internal accounting of actual wastes dumped over a fifteen-year period. The volume of such material was considerably less than the agency had attributed to these corporations, but the recordkeeping seemed unassailable. In response, the agency reopened its investigation to find additional PRPs to explain the large quantity of waste material found.

On the other hand, a huge, multinational transportation company recently acquiesced in responsibility for a larger quantity of wastes than it had actually dumped at a Superfund site in a western state. Ironically, the transportation company had retained its dump tickets and receipts over the course of three decades. Unfortunately, the EPA found these dump tickets to be sporadic, and presumed that others were missing. The tickets, for example, accounted, in a given year, for wastes hauled in February, May, August, September, and November, but not for the remaining months. Rather than assume that the transportation company had retained all of its dump receipts, the EPA assumed that many of the receipts were lost, and assigned to the company responsibility for an average quantity of wastes dumped during those months for which no receipts appeared on file. Because the company had not established a records management policy, it could not convince the agency that the receipts had not been haphazardly kept.

ESTABLISHING AN ENVIRONMENTAL ARCHIVES

Having such tremendous incentive to establish an environmental archive, corporations also have the opportunity to avail themselves of consulting firms that have experience in locating, identifying, sorting, and keying pertinent internal documents. Firms well rounded in historical documentation are ideal for the task of identifying and locating some of the disparate and possibly extinct types of source material which will contain the essential data. These types of historical records may range from accounts payable files to bills of lading to agency permits to internal memoranda describing processing or disposal procedures.

In some corporations, developing an environmental archives will be more difficult than in others, simply because of the state of extant historical records. Important information may have to be extracted from apparently unrelated source material, and this is where the professional historian has the opportunity for creative investigation. Old tax returns, for example, can itemize waste material in claiming a business loss and may prove an important source of disposal information. In some cases, the historian may find it necessary to investigate external records and integrate them into corporate memory. Some hauling companies, for example, may cooperate with former customers and open old records for review and retrieval. On occasion, the investigator may find missing data on file in an agency archives. In California, for example, the Regional Water Pollution Control Boards regulated much dumping activity during the 1950s and, in doing so, required quarterly reports from waste haulers, detailing the source, nature, and quantity of the wastes hauled. Many of those reports remain available, although they, too, were not always filed systematically, and some are therefore difficult to locate.

As a first step, then, the historical consultants will survey extant records and classify them as to type of document, such as ledger sheet; contract; invoice; purchase order; procedural manual, etc. Systematically sampling the records thus classified, the historians will identify the files richest in the following kinds of information:

1. names and quantities of chemical products purchased or sold
2. types and volumes of chemicals purchased or sold
3. costs of chemicals or chemical products purchased or sold
4. type, quantity, and whereabouts of fuel deliveries
5. quantity of fuel(s) dispensed
6. waste disposal contractors
7. waste disposal expenditures
8. composition and quantity of wastes
9. predisposal waste treatments
10. date and findings of public agency inspections
11. date and nature of any abatement measures
12. name and address of maintenance contractors

The record sampling technique allows the historians to tailor the information collection effort to suit the records of the individual corporation and to identify areas where it will be necessary to augment the internal data. Using the results of the record sampling effort, the historians will develop a triage system, supervise the information collection effort, and design a cross-indexed data base that also includes a method for document retrieval.

In addition, any corporate archives of historic hazardous substances data the consultants create should dovetail with a record management system designed to maintain the company in compliance with current environmental documentation requirements. Today, for example, under the Emergency Planning and Community Right-to-Know provisions of SARA, companies that use or store certain quantities of certain listed chemicals (the EPA's list currently contains almost 1,100 such chemicals) have a number of federal permit and reporting requirements, and they are likely to have state and local reporting requirements as well. EPA Form R is entitled the "Toxic Chemical Release Inventory Reporting Form," and it requires detailed information about current operations at a facility, including data on waste minimization and waste treatment efforts. Another federal law, the Resource Conservation and Recovery Act, created "cradle-to grave" documentation requirements of all treatment and disposal of hazardous wastes. In light of these new laws, corporate environmental archives should also accommodate current compliance records, anticipating that these government-developed or mandated forms are apt to become the most appropriate records for developing PRP information in any future liability defense.

The effective environmental archives should thus permit easy access to hazardous substance and waste records from the era prior to EPA regulation and to analogous records generated through EPA and state and local regulation. In addition, the system should record changes in the documentary record as required updating occurs.

In general, then, the methods for creating a corporate archives of environmental data are analogous to those employed for other management or litigation records. If the consultants accurately anticipate the data required for current and future toxic waste investigations, collect the data systematically, design a flexible data base, and insure that the documents are retrievable, then the archives will become an invaluable corporate asset.

NOTES

1. 42 U.S.C. Sections 9601–9657 (1980).
2. Pub. L. No. 99-499, 100 Stat. 1613 (1986).
3. *U.S. v. A & F Materials Co., Inc.* D.C. Ill. 1984, 578 F. Supp. 1249.
4. See, e. g., New York, City of v. Exxon, 633 F. Supp. 609, 16 *Environmental Law Reporter* 20850 (S.D.N.Y. 1986).
5. Kenneth P. Cohen, "Allocation of Superfund Cleanup Costs Among Potentially Responsible Parties: The Role of Binding Arbitration," 18 *Environmental Law Reporter* 19158 (May 1988).
6. Resource Conservation and Recovery Act, 42 U.S.C Section 6973 et seq. (1976), acronym RCRA, created recordkeeping requirements for the treatment, storage, and disposal of hazardous wastes.

Richard Katz is the special assistant for information systems and administrative services of the University of California system. He is currently working with the University of California's Presidential Transition Team and UCLA's chancellor on a variety of strategic management initiatives. Prior to joining the University of California in 1982, where he was responsible for designing and implementing one of the nation's first electronic document registry systems, Katz was records manager and archivist for a number of private and public organizations. He earned his bachelor's degree from the University of Pittsburgh and an M.B.A. from the University of California at Los Angeles.

Victoria A. Davis is currently an executive assistant budget officer for Fermi National Accelerator Laboratory. From 1978 to 1987, she was archivist and records manager at Lawrence Berkeley Laboratory and was responsible for establishing their first archives and updating an ongoing Records Management Program. Prior to that, she served as archivist of the City College of New York and as director of the Department of Archives, History, and Policy Information for the American Medical Association.

THE IMPACT OF AUTOMATION ON OUR CORPORATE MEMORY

Richard N. Katz and Victoria A. Davis

The good news for information management practitioners is that the U.S. economy is now viewed by many as an information economy. Over one and one-half million information professionals currently manage the 70 billion new pieces of information that are produced in this country every year. By the year 2000, recorded knowledge will be accruing four times faster than the human population.[1]

The emergence of this information economy may present a number of exciting possibilities for those of us currently responsible for managing the nation's records, libraries, databases, and archives. As with most "opportunities," it will not be possible to predict accurately the course of future changes, and tomorrow's information management leaders will be those individuals who demonstrate today the ability to assess technologies, take risks, and keep uppermost in mind the basic goals and objectives of information management.

Simply stated, information management's basic goal is the rapid delivery of useful information to the right people in a cost-effective manner. This goal is based on several assumptions: (1) not all information is useful; (2) different people need different information; (3) time is of the essence;

Reprinted with permission from *ARMA Records Management Quarterly* published by the Association of Records Managers and Administrators International.

(4) money is of the essence; and (5) not everyone has the "need to know" to gain access to information.

This basic goal, and its underlying assumptions, have a tendency to focus on measurable bottom-line results. Indeed our ability to "sell" records management to our management and users is based historically on financial performance. This focus has resulted in an occupational eagerness to implement new systems for the efficient management of information resources, with a concomitant devaluation of our role as the *conservators* of strategic (e.g., vital and historical) information resources. In recognition of this fact, responsibility for "archives" is typically tucked away quietly near the bottom of a typical records management job description and data processing professionals have co-opted the term to refer to electronic data requiring retention for five to ten years.

The purpose of this article is not to discourage the implementation of newer and more efficient automated systems, but to identify potential longer-term problems associated with these systems and to prescribe a possible remedy. Information management professionals must continually remind themselves that technology is the engine that drives our information economy, it is not the driver. With the right rolling stock, some analytical road maps and a good sense of direction, information managers should be able to anticipate and avoid the large number of road hazards facing them.

TECHNOLOGICAL NEED

Manual systems are collapsing under the weight of their own paper. The increasing requirements for easy access to perishable information in a useable format are causing manual systems to become obsolete. In the coming years, information managers must anticipate the replacement of paper-based manual systems with automated systems. The technologies that will make this replacement possible include: (1) mainframe computer hardware and software developments that will support the development of very large databases; (2) electronic imaging systems, including optical character recognition, FAX and other raster-type conversion technologies that will facilitate the conversion of printed text to machine-readable data; (3) intelligent printers and copiers and sophisticated print on demand capabilities; (4) powerful workstations and personal computers that will promote the increased distributed use *and management* of electronic information; (5) optical mass memory systems to store digital information and compressed images; and (6) data communications technologies, in particular network infrastructure development and continued improvements in the price and performance of fiber optics.

Library holdings on the technical, sociological, and administrative aspects of these various technologies are growing at an astronomical rate. Although it is not feasible to recapitulate this literature here, it will be helpful to illustrate the issues involved by focusing on the technological area most likely to have enormous impact on information managers—optical memories.

INPUT, a highly respected information industry consulting firm based in California's Silicon Valley, stated in 1983 that "the potential of optical memories is more than another step in the evolution of computer storage media. Optical storage could provide a fundamental shift, not only in the nature of business transactions, but in the very recordkeeping of the human race. Comparable shifts in history were the introduction of papyrus in ancient Egypt and the printing of the Gutenberg Bible in the 15th century."[2]

INPUT goes on, in the same report, to predict that:

1. Optical disk systems are expected to become ten times cheaper than paper within the next 5 years;
2. By the mid-1980s optical memory will exhibit significant cost advantages (vis-à-vis paper and micrographics) for document storage of information requiring frequent access;
3. By the late 1980s it will be difficult to justify the retention of paper documents except for small, personal files;
4. Optical disks will be cheaper than paper for archival storage of data and information will therefore be discardable if the disks on which it is stored cannot be reused.

Even discounting these specific predictions with the benefit of our hindsight five years later, still, many information management professionals have come to incorporate optical memory technologies somewhere in their planning activities. The key question of how well we have planned for this eventuality remains unanswered by much of the professional literature.

QUESTIONS TO BE ANSWERED

The convergence of optical memory technologies with other information systems is likely to place information management professionals behind the eight ball. The increased integration of the technologies mentioned above will dramatically impact the following areas:

1. *What is to be automated?* This is a question traditionally addressed by functional management and information systems (IS) management. Will records management and archives professionals lose their role in providing cost/benefit analyses (as with micrographics) and in establishing standards as the cost of creating and storing digital information decreases?
2. *The end-user as information manager.* The increased distribution of computing power and local storage of data will enable end users to build, maintain, and "archive" information of strategic importance. Who in

the organization will develop and oversee standards governing the access, security, and integrity of the data in these systems, particularly as records in these systems become the "record copy"?

3. *The IS life cycle and media shelf life.* Much is being written about the "archival" characteristics of optical storage media. Less is written about the IS life cycle that practically guarantees the obsolescence of any new information system in five to seven years. Who will establish the standards to ensure that strategic electronic data will be retrievable in 10 years? In 100 years?

4. *Information systems are communications systems.* Increasingly sophisticated networks will enable us to "publish" business records and other data. Who will oversee these activities with a view to the copyright, trade secret, and legal discovery ramifications?

5. *Managing end-user expectations.* The new technologies will create the capability to deliver smaller and smaller units of information on demand. Information management professionals will no longer be rewarded for pulling five boxes quickly from a record center, but will be expected to deliver pieces of relevant information from diverse data depositories. Success in meeting these increased requirements will depend on the sophistication of our retrieval tools, not on effective warehousing skills.

There will obviously be a number of other impacts arising in the wake of implementing these new technologies. The trends and issues identified above can be summarized as follows: (1) the new technologies will enable us to store and retrieve more information faster and cheaper; (2) the responsibility for managing corporate (and governmental) information will migrate increasingly to end users; (3) documents of different types will be stored and manipulated electronically; and (4) more information will be "distributed" or "communicated" by electronic means.

Does this mean that we are soon to pass through the gates to information heaven? Anyone who has followed our progress toward the "paperless office" knows that this is not the case. 3M Vice President D. W. McArthur recently observed that one reason that corporations' electronic document-handling needs are not being met is that "the OA [office automation] process has been placed in the hands of computer people, who are making purchasing and design decisions without the assistance and input of the document professionals."[3] The message for information management professionals regarding electronic records is a familiar one: (1) the more information you store, the harder it is to find the information you need; (2) the more information you give end users to manage, the higher the incidence of information degradation, memory loss, and security breaches; and (3) the easier you make it to "communicate" information, the higher your exposure to legal discovery actions and the greater the risk of communicating misinformation. When entire libraries come to be stored on-line, we also can expect to put our copyright laws and policies through some trials by fire.

THE RECORDS MANAGER'S ROLE

Because records managers and archivists are familiar with most of the issues left unresolved by the emerging technologies, these professionals should play an essential role in the design and oversight of information activities in the decade ahead. The ability of these professionals to fill a niche in "data management" will depend on their incorporation of an increasingly interdisciplinary approach to their activities.[4] As the Associated Information Managers (AIM) suggests, records managers and archivists must define themselves as "members of the management team responsible for acquiring and developing the information content and technology resources suited to the needs of their organization."

Archivists and records managers must extend the scope of their skills to include the methodologies of librarianship and information systems management, as well as those of each other if they are to ensure the security, retrievability, reliability, and permanence of electronic information. This may be difficult. As Frank Burke, formerly the Acting Archivist of the United States, observed, "[Archivists] are raised professionally in a tradition of uniqueness. We invoke uniqueness as both a rationale for action and an excuse for inaction. But we have made the mistake of extending the concept of the uniqueness of our records to a uniqueness in the techniques of managing them."[5]

Assuming we are successful in amalgamating the skills and techniques of these related professions, what role can information management professionals of this new type hope to play? A useful approach to this question should include a skills inventory of the future information manager:

1. Indexing, cataloguing, and circulation control. Librarians, and to a lesser degree, archivists and records managers understand the need for authority control to promote efficient information retrieval. Large data bases will require extremely sophisticated access tools (e.g., thesauri, dictionaries, etc.) and network requirements will depend on the development and implementation of document standards and protocol standards.
2. Systems analysis, including cost/benefit analysis. Records managers, wherever their placement in the organization, are natural systems analysts. This orientation in addition to their experience with users' information needs makes them invaluable team members in new system design.
3. Information systems management. Skills in this area include technology assessment, systems analysis, and awareness of organizational computing requirements and constraints. IS professionals are strongly versed and sympathetic with information security and integrity requirements. These people also have a stronger hand organizationally and budgetarily than most information management professionals.

4. Archives administration. This uniquely positioned professional group understands corporate information requirements at the highest level. This group has developed strong skills in information appraisal and represents the social "conscience" of information management.

Any one person possessing this battery of skills and a broad organizational perspective may lead the profession in the next decade. Operationally, in an environment where the traditional document storage and retrieval functions have been automated, such an individual could participate in many aspects of system design. Indexing skills will enable the information manager to identify and articulate standards for keyword control. Knowledge of the library document and network standards will be essential where data are to be exchanged on existing national networks. The archival perspective should be incorporated at the stage when new systems are designed to ensure that hardware, software, format, and network standards are configured in such a way as to guarantee that electronic data can be converted when systems are upgraded. The new information manager will work with a team in developing security and access standards to ensure that sensitive information is secure, reliable, and auditable. The new information manager will, of course, ensure that retention requirements for electronic information are complied with.

In short, the records manager or archivist of the future must assume a more visible role in information systems management if the corporate memory is to be trusted or retained. For those of us already reporting in the MIS line, the conclusions drawn above are already self-evident. For those of us not reporting to MIS, we should seek to identify managers and professionals who are making the design and equipment decisions that will have an impact on our ability to manage electronic information and offer our services. With success, information managers should strive to become members of the IS planning and design team and should endeavor to establish an audit role for themselves in the design and purchase processes.

ADDITIONAL EFFORTS

On the professional level, there are other things we can do. Because new technologies emerge faster than our literature can summarize and because many of these technologies have tremendous information management impacts and continually demand the development of new standards and guidelines, professional associations such as ARMA should consider the establishment of an interassociational task group to assess the impact of new technologies on information management and to promote some of the inter-disciplinary dialogue discussed above. Such a group would be well positioned to identify areas of technological impact, to identify resulting issues, to discuss the need for standards and identify appropriate organizations to develop such standards. Such a group might also provide our professional associations with some direction in regard to the emerging and evolving public policy vis-à-vis electronic information. This area may prove to be a new and exciting area of involvement for information management professionals. It would include the development of policies and laws to: (1) preserve the evidentiary value of electronic records; (2) ensure the preservation of a meaningful historical electronic record; (3) safeguard the privacy of individuals about whom electronic records refer; (4) facilitate access rights of individuals under state and federal law; (5) safeguard proprietary information on behalf of our employers; and (6) comply with appropriate copyright laws. The need for such professional cooperation was recognized recently with the establishment, in 1989, of the Coalition for Networked Information. The coalition, formed by the Association of Research Libraries (ARL), CAUSE, and EDUCOM, is working with member institutions in the higher education and technology vendor communities to promote the creation of and access to information resources in networked environments in order to enrich scholarship and to enhance academic productivity.

The challenge of managing these new technologies is before us. Information management professionals must now decide by which yardstick we'll measure our contribution, the cubic foot, or the bit.

NOTES

1. Edward Weldon, "Challenges of Change," *American Archivist* 46 (Spring 1983): 128. See also the remarks of the U.S. Bureau of the Census, Vincent P. Barabba, "Demographic Change and the Public Work Force," prepared for the 2nd Public Management Research Conference on the Changing Character of the Public Work Force, Washington, D.C., (Nov. 18, 1980).
2. INPUT, *Optical Mass Memories* (Mt. View, Calif: 1983).
3. D. W. McArthur, "Automation: Is It Off Schedule?", *The Office* (July 1985). See also the observations of the Committee on the Records of Government which warned "the United States is in danger of losing its memory," in *Report of the Committee on the Records of Government*, Council on Library Resources, Washington, D.C., (March, 1985).
4. Jake Knoppers, "Integrating Technologies—Integrating Disciplines?", *Records Management Quarterly* 17 (Jan. 1983), 5–7. See also Margaret S. Childs, "Reflections on Cooperation Among Professions," *American Archivist* 46 (Summer 1983), 286–292. Ms. Childs observed that "the time is not far in the future when libraries and archives will begin to fall together because not only will they be handling information conveyed by a great variety of mediums but also the methodological distinctions between the control of printed matter and control applied to other kinds of documentation will cease to have any meaning when the same videodisc may well contain printed texts, still photographs, moving pictures. . . and organizational records. Now what kind of catalogue record should that have?"
5. Frank G. Burke, "Archival Cooperation," *American Archivist* 46 (Summer 1983): 294.

PART III
THE CORPORATE ARCHIVIST:
PROFESSIONAL CONCERNS IN
A CHANGING ENVIRONMENT

THE CORPORATE ARCHIVIST:
PROFESSIONAL CONCERNS IN A
CHANGING ENVIRONMENT

The profession of archivist in the United States is still relatively new and uncommon. That of corporate archivist is still more so. Frequently such a position is defined in terms of what it is not—not a records manager, for example, but not an ordinary step up the executive ladder either. In the business world, the archivist frequently doubles as company historian; occasionally archives are attached to corporate libraries, but their functions do not coincide. Increasingly, however, management of a successful corporate archives involves aspects of all these jobs and more.

In the first selection for this section, David R. Smith takes us through the brief history of the development of business archives. He reminds us it was not until the birth of the National Archives in the 1930s that professionals, through the Society of American Archivists, began to take steps to set standards for practice. While SAA had a business archives committee as early as 1938, it was only in the next decade that a few companies took the lead in establishing a professionally-managed archives program. Even then growth was slow until the early 1970s, when the field entered a period of unprecedented growth. Speculating about the reasons for this development, Smith suggests a connection between archives and several other phenomena, especially the popularity of anniversary celebrations, such as the Bicentennial of the American Revolution, or the increasing need for historical documents in litigation proceedings. Still, the place of corporate archives in American business is far from assured, he warns us, and even the very best work can be threatened by a management that perceives them as an unnecessary frill.

Philip F. Mooney outlines how a corporation might approach staffing a new archives program, emphasizing the wisdom in hiring a qualified and experienced professional.

The first generation of archivists, according to David R. Smith, was largely drawn from the ranks of historians who learned to adapt to needs of archives, both public and private. In addressing the problem of an increasing need for standards in the education of today's archivists, Frederick J. Stielow makes it clear that the future will be quite different. Two factors, he argues, are having an irreversible impact on the role and status of the corporate archivist of the future. One is the increasing computerization of business records which, in the last decade or so, has led to a new perception by management of information as a resource. Another is the increasing scope and complexity of archival education. Stielow outlines how graduate training programs evolved during the 1970s and 1980s and shows how these developments coincided with an increasing sense of professionalism on the part of archivists. He ends with an assessment of recent efforts at accreditation of degree programs and certification of individuals.

Many of the recently developed degree programs for the field of archives contain a substantial on-the-job training component. Such opportunities can be particularly helpful to students and employers alike, for nowhere is there yet a complete program in the area of corporate archives education that offers specialized training in this field. Anne Millbrooke has described for us an internship program she has offered for approximately a decade at the Archives and Historical Resource Center of United Technologies, a large international corporation that includes among its divisions such well-known manufacturing companies as Otis Elevator and Carrier Air Conditioning. Carefully noting the responsibilities of both student and employer, she outlines the progress of an intern through a typical program (a sample schedule is included) and suggests various criteria by which success can be measured. Programs like those at United Technologies and elsewhere have the additional advantage of offering a means by which the steadily evolving needs of employers—in an age of rapid change in information technology—can be monitored by educators. While maintaining such programs is never routine, decisions regarding them will always be made with their cost-effectiveness in view. Still, employers and educators, who both hold a stake in the continued production of professional archivists who have the skills appropriate to today's demands, will do well to nurture the internship as a useful tool.

Nancy M. Merz puts less stress on the potential competing interests of archives and records managers than on their need for interdependence. Like Katz and Davis in the preceding section, she also calls for increased cooperation among professional associations representing these fields. As Merz analyzes the historical development of both archives and records management, she points out that the latter have been much more readily adaptable to the practice and language of the business world than have archivists, who maintained close ties to the history community and to the academy. Drawing from her own experience with the Texas Local Records Department and later as a consultant to a multinational corporation, she assesses the impact of changing technology and stresses the need for the combined skills of both archivists and records managers in meeting challenges which lie ahead. As technological advancements occur, Merz argues, archivists and records managers will become increasingly dependent on each other to maintain control of records and information systems and also to establish standards and procedures that will ensure quality work.

What is the appropriate education for the corporate archivists of the twenty-first century? What will be their primary professional loyalty? How will archivists relate to others in organizations where they work? to changes in technology? Will archivists view themselves as a distinct profession or as one type of information manager? The answers to these questions are not clear, but it is certain that the coming decades will bring with them change.

David R. Smith joined The Walt Disney Company as the director of the Archives in 1970. He holds the B.A. in history and an M.A. in Library Science from the University of California at Berkeley and is an active member of the Society of American Archivists (and for two years chairman of its Business Archives Committee), the Society of California Archivists, and the Association for State and Local History. He also has written extensively on Disney history, with a regular column in The Disney Channel Magazine *and numerous articles in such publications as* Disney News, Starlog, Manuscripts, Millimeter, American Archivist, *and* California Historical Quarterly.

AN HISTORICAL LOOK AT BUSINESS ARCHIVES

David R. Smith

As historical and research institutions go, business archives are a relatively recent phenomenon. One hundred years ago, when business and industry in the United States had left the havoc of the Civil War behind them and were growing at a tremendous pace, there were no business archives. Three decades later, the call to the United States to help friendly nations put a stop to the ambitions of Kaiser Wilhelm in Europe led to a major growth in industries preparing war materiel, but still no business archives were established. Two more decades passed before an industrialist had the foresight to begin saving his company's historical files in systematic fashion.

This lack of archival development was not confined solely to business archives. Many of us forget that the National Archives building in Washington, D.C. was constructed in 1934—that is still recent history! Groups of historians had taken part in a long and arduous struggle to have legislation passed that would establish the National Archives. When they finally succeeded, it marked the beginning of formal archival history in America.

One must remember that in those early days when archives were first coming into their own, there were not only few archives, there were no archivists. The first archives established were staffed by historians and others who were trained in the methods of historical research. It was during this gestation period that the Society of American Archivists was organized, and early steps were taken to establish a set of standards for uniform archival practices to cope with the astonishing quantity of records that was growing by leaps and bounds.

It was not until 1950, with passage of the Federal Records Act, that the National Archives finally began to deal seriously with records management. The archivists had finally come to realize that many of the records

Reprinted with permission from *American Archivist* Vol. 45, 1982, 273–78.

they were storing were not of permanent value. But this realization was not unique to the National Archives.

While these birth and growing pains were being felt within the federal government, other archives were undergoing a parallel process of growth. These included not only city, county, and state archives, but also archives of businesses, churches, and universities.

With a greater awareness on the part of historians of the importance of business history, businesses began to receive encouragement to preserve their important records. When SAA's Business Archives Committee was created in 1938, one government archivist wrote in the *American Archivist*, "The historian who seeks to interpret our contemporary life without taking into account the shaping forces of modern business will but touch the fringe of his subject. For more than a generation people have spoken of two capitals, Washington and Wall Street. The relations between these giant concentrations of power are of immense significance to the people. We are careful to preserve the records of one capital but have sadly neglected the records of the other."[1]

Businesses in this country began to have real problems with records after World War I, during which expanded facilities and government contracts had generated ever-increasing amounts of paperwork. Book-keepers and eventually records managers were called upon to handle the crush. Recommendations for disposal of large amounts of little-used records were made by the records managers, and soon a number of companies had set up specific records retention and disposal systems.

Because records managers seemed to be interested primarily in disposing of records as fast as they could get releases from the departments involved, some historians, and, thankfully, some business executives too, began to wonder if this wholesale disposal of records was perhaps being carried out a little too quickly.

One of the first executives to do anything about his company's records was Harvey S. Firestone. He and his son, Harvey S. Firestone, Jr., began to fear that some records of permanent value were not being retained. Not only were they planning a company history, but they believed also "that certain records would be of value to management for reference in making decisions regarding current business problems as they arose."[2] They realized that if steps were not taken soon, it would be too late.

To ensure that valuable and useful records were safeguarded and preserved through proper evaluation, the Firestone Tire and Rubber Co., in 1943 became the first company to hire an archivist and begin a comprehensive archives program in cooperation with the company's records manager. This first business archivist was William D. Overman, who had for a number of years been curator of history and state archivist at the Ohio State Archaeological and Historical Society and who later served as president of SAA.[3]

While Harvey Firestone and his staff showed great foresight, their lead was not immediately followed by other companies. One basic problem was that neither librarians, nor scholars, nor businessmen had decided *where* business records should be preserved. Some thought that these files should be in libraries. While some large libraries did have good collections of business records, mostly of defunct companies, the librarians began to realize that where there had once been small businesses, there now were large corporations and even conglomerates composed of several corporations. The collections of their business records were becoming so large and unwieldy that the libraries could no longer afford to either house or maintain them. Large business collections were collecting dust, unprocessed, in the libraries' most distant and seldom-visited storerooms. Arthur H. Cole, librarian of the Baker Library at Harvard, wrote an article in the *Journal of Economic History* in 1945 in which he recommended that businesses preserve their own records.[4]

During the 1940s, very little was accomplished along these lines, with only a few companies—including Time, Inc., Armstrong Cork, INA, and Eastman Kodak—joining Firestone's lead in starting archival programs. Businesses were not convinced of the wisdom of preserving their historically important files. There was only one area where some businesses were saving their history, and this was in company museums. These began around the turn of the century, long before business archives, and by 1943, when a definitive book was written on the subject, 80 companies in the United States had museums of their own.[5] Some of these museums would later be incorporated into archival programs.

The 1950s saw a slight renewal of interest, and companies such as Ford, Sears Roebuck, New York Life Insurance, Eli Lilly, Procter and Gamble, Bank of America, and Coca-Cola began archives. And yet when a survey was taken in 1958, fewer than 12 large companies reported that they had archivists on their staffs.

William Overman, Firestone's archivist, in his presidential address to the Society of American Archivists in 1958, said, "There are literally hundreds of business corporations in the United States that can afford to set up their own archives if they are shown how to do it or if they are persuaded that a program for the proper care of their permanent records will pay them great dividends in the long run."[6] The problem was that no one was doing the persuading. It was not coming out of the historical profession, and it was not coming out of the archival profession.

In the 1960s, business archives went into the doldrums. Only four major business archives were begun. A questionnaire distributed in 1964 to 402 firms elicited a response that only 10 percent were preserving records to any degree, and only a few of these had an archivist in charge. The SAA disbanded its Business Archives Committee and threw business archivists into a group consisting of business, urban, and labor archives. This created strange bedfellows because the latter two were involved with social concerns while the business archives were involved with economic concerns.

The publication in 1969 of a *Directory of Business Archives* by the SAA signaled the birth of a new era. A questionnaire had been sent to 700 firms, with 133 reporting that they had at least some semblance of an archives, even if it consisted only of one file drawer in the office of the secretary to the chairman of the board. Of the 133 firms, only 13 reported having a full-time archivist on their staff, although to that number could be added nine historians and one museum director.

Perhaps, we may think as we reach around to give ourselves a pat on the back, the very act of sending this questionnaire to 700 companies made business executives start to think: "What *are* we doing without history?" "Are some of our files historically important?" "Should we be considering starting an archives program?"

Of course, there were many reasons for the rebirth in the early 1970s of interest in business archives. The nostalgia craze made instant antiques or "collectibles" out of the relatively recent products of many of our companies. Universities were turning out large numbers of history graduates who, finding jobs scarce in the field of education, helped convince some businesses that they could be useful in an archives program. The U.S. Bicentennial celebrations on the horizon brought renewed interest in history. Many companies were reaching major anniversaries and needed organized collections so that their histories could be written. And, lawsuits against companies were becoming all the more common, making easy access to historical files necessary to company attorneys. Whatever the reason, beginning in 1970 there was a veritable flood of new business archives.

I can speak from personal experience about Walt Disney Productions. The company had been thinking about what to do with its historical files in 1969. Overtures were made by UCLA to have the records deposited in their library, but this was deemed unfeasible. Not only was there more material than UCLA could possibly handle, but the company needed constant access to the material and needed also to maintain the confidentiality of business secrets. I was hired by Disney as a consultant, and I made good use of the just-published *Directory of Business Archives* to send inquiries about procedures and policies to other archivists. Out of this work came a proposal for setting up an archives within the company, which was soon implemented.

During the 1970s, Disney was joined by a number of other companies, including International Harvester, Anheuser-Busch, Corning Glass, Weyerhaeuser, Wells Fargo Bank, Deere & Co., Gerber Products, Los Angeles Times, and Atlantic Richfield. Within a decade, the number of business archives in the country nearly doubled, and, even more significantly, the number of business archivists quadrupled. Still we are a rare breed, but we are no longer in danger of extinction, which had been real possibility just ten years ago.

The Business Archives Committee was reinstated by SAA, eventually to be superseded by a professional affinity group, which now has 176 members. The 1975 edition of SAA's *Directory of Business Archives* listed 196 archives, with 30 archivists, and the more recent 1980 edition listed 200 archives, with 60 archivists.

Business archives have come into their own in the last decade, not only with the accelerated growth in numbers, but with the outreach efforts of present members of the profession. In 1974, Edie Hedlin, while at the Ohio Historical Society, prepared an extremely useful tool to send to businesses contemplating the beginning of an archives program. This business archives manual was later revised, published, and distributed under the auspices of SAA.[7] SAA has also increased the number of sessions of business archival interest at its annual meetings and sponsored several in-depth workshops on business archives in different parts of the country.

We must not be made complacent, however, by all these recent successes. Not only do we need to continue to make other companies aware of the value of an archival program, but we must continue the hard sell within our own companies. With changes constantly being made at the middle and top levels of management, we need to continue our educational efforts to prove the value of an archives. In the past, some business archives—perish the thought—have been known to vanish. This can happen when a company's management has a change of heart, when the company is bought out or merges with another, or even when the founder of the archives retires or dies. Executives must continually be made aware of the value of their archives, so they do not think that as soon as the company's centennial history has been written, the archives can be disbanded, dispensed with, or destroyed.

One sad situation that occurred recently in Hollywood can be cited as an example. A well-known animated cartoon studio was approached by a young animation historian and film buff with a detailed program for the establishment of an archives. His plan caught the fancy of the company's founders, who hired the young man as archivist. He immediately proceeded to collect from warehouses the most important animation artwork prepared by the company over several decades, including samples from each film or series. These drawings, celluloids, and backgrounds were carefully preserved, while all the remainder was destroyed. Various other historical files were gathered, including samples of licensed books and merchandise, and the company's founders took pride in showing off the archives to visitors. After about six months, however, the large conglomerate that owned the company learned of the archives and deemed it an unnecessary expense. Not only was the archivist summarily fired, but all of the artwork and files that he had gathered were collected and destroyed.

We have seen many changes take place in the field of business archives since Harvey Firestone made his move back in 1943. Much of the growth that has taken place can be attributed, at least in part, to the greater awareness of the value of business history. In 1964, Professor Ralph Hidy of Harvard spoke on the importance of business in the history of our country: "During the past 200 years, no other single group in our society has been more influential in raising our standards of living, in setting the direction of institutional and social changes, in affecting our national policies and international relations. Only by understanding what businessmen have done, and their ways of doing it, can we get a realistic appraisal of the broad history of the American people."[8] In the past four decades, businesses have shown that they can help preserve some of that history themselves, and they have set examples for other companies to follow in the future.

Establishment of Business Archives—Chronology

1943—Firestone	1969—Educational Testing
1944—INA	Service
1945—	1970—Walt Disney Productions;
1946—Time, Inc.	Ford Foundation
1947—Armstrong Cork	1971—International Harvester;
1948—	Anheuser-Busch
1949—Alcoa; Lever Brothers;	1972—United Technologies
Eastman Kodak	1973—Corning Glass
1950—Texaco	Works
1951—Ford	1974—Weyerhauser; Nationwide
1952—	Insurance
1953—	1975—Wells Fargo Bank; Chase
1954—Rockefeller Family	Manhattan Bank
1955—Sears Roebuck; New	1976—Deere & Co.; Gerber
York Life Insurance	Products
1956—Eli Lilly	1977—Georgia Pacific Co.
1957—Procter & Gamble	1978—Los Angeles Times;
1958—Bank of America;	Nabisco
Coca-Cola	1979—Atlantic Richfield; New
1959—	York Stock Exchange;
1960—	J. Walter Thompson
1961—IBM	1980—General Mills
1962—	1983—Kraft
1963—	1984—Texas Instruments
1964—	Incorporated
1965—Gulf Oil	1986—Sporting News
1966—	1988—King Ranch; The
1967—	Aerospace Corporation
1968—Chicago Board of Trade	1991—Phillips Petroleum

NOTES

1. Oliver W. Holmes, "The Evaluation and Preservation of Business Archives," *American Archivist* 1 (October 1938): 171–85.
2. Quoted in William D. Overman, "The Pendulum Swings," *American Archivist* 22 (January 1959): 4.
3. Overman had worked with the Firestone family since 1937, while still at the Historical Society, on the cataloging of historical papers. See William D. Overman, "The Firestone Archives and Library," *American Archivist* 16 (October 1953): 305–309.
4. Arthur H. Cole, "Business Manuscripts: A Pressing Problem," *Journal of Economic History* 5 (May 1945): 43–59.
5. Lawrence Vail Coleman, *Company Museums* (Washington, D.C.: The American Association of Museums, 1943).

6. Overman, "The Pendulum Swings," 9.
7. Edie Hedlin, *Ohio Business Archives Manual* (Columbus: Ohio Historical Society, 1974); idem., *Business Archives: An Introduction* (Chicago: Society of American Archivists, 1978).
8. Ralph W. Hidy, "Business Archives: Introductory Remarks," *American Archivist* 29 (January 1966): 34.

For a biographical sketch of Philip F. Mooney, see his essay "The Practice of History in Corporate America: Business Archives in the United States," elsewhere in this book.

RESOURCES FOR CORPORATIONS: AN ARCHIVAL PRIMER

Philip F. Mooney

At first glance, the objective seems reasonable and straightforward. Your company has decided to establish an archival program to deal with its historical records. But now, a few glitches have begun to appear in what seemed to be a simple program. Nobody really knows what constitutes a historically important record, and, worse still, the physical location of the material remains shrouded in mystery. While there is a general consensus that history has value and that "heritage" plays an important role in the definition of a corporate culture, the precise details of how an archival program should work and what contributions it should make to corporate goals and objectives are much more difficult to pinpoint and define.

Then too there is the question of cost. In an environment where every corporate operation must justify its existence through a rigorous budgetary analysis, how does history fit into the equation? In addition there is the question of headcount. If "lean and mean" is a standard element in the vocabulary of your human resources managers, does it make sense to bring in an outsider to direct an archival program, when good old Bill Johnson, a thirty-five year employee without a real job, has always taken an interest in company history and possesses a very extensive personal collection of widgets, ephemera, and memorabilia. Alternatively, logic suggests that there must be a number of turn-key consultant groups who can solve all of these problems in a week or two at most, leaving behind, when they depart, a beautifully cataloged collection that can function as a self-service operation.

While this scenario may be overdrawn, it outlines the myriad of problems and decisions that corporations face when reviewing the potential utility of an international archival program. Unfortunately, many businesses look for a quick-fix solution when evaluating programs with historical implications and do not apply the same principles of research and analysis that govern their actions in the marketing and technical areas. Yet for an archival program to yield both quantitative and qualitative benefits to the parent body, corporations need to understand the nature of the archival world, the basic principles that underlie most archival work, and the end products that archivists produce and manage. With this basic understanding and frame of reference, the corporation can make rea-

An earlier version of this chapter was collected in *Proceedings of Preserving the History of the Aerospace Industry*, a Conference at the Smithsonian Institution, 1990.

soned decisions regarding the structure of its archival function and the defined role it holds within the organization.

One of the first places to start the research process is to survey the professional literature. The Society of American Archivists (SAA), based in Chicago, is the national professional association for archivists in all fields, and its publications, meetings, committees, and programs are the primary sources for useful information on the development, form, and content of North American business archives. Though somewhat dated in terms of modern practice and technological developments, Edie Hedlin's manual on Business Archives, published by SAA in 1978, remains the most comprehensive American treatment of this subject. An Australian booklet, entitled *Managing Business Archives*, contains published papers from a 1986 seminar and offers some interesting insights from an international perspective and expands on many of the concepts first outlined in the Hedlin manual.

A special edition of *The American Archivist*, dedicated to business archives and published in 1982, provides a sound overview to the field and includes suggested guidelines for business archives. It is still available in a reprinted format from SAA. A broader view of all associated archival literature related to business archives and records management can be found in a bibliography, compiled by Karen Benedict, that SAA has published and updated several times since its initial appearance in 1981.

Like all disciplines, the informal contacts and direct interviews with allied bodies often prove more useful than a bookshelf of reference works. Successive editions of *The Directory of Business Archives in the United States and Canada*, published by SAA, have enabled institutions to identify like bodies and to network with them sharing similar problems and approaches to archival work, though the most recent published directory appeared in 1990.

While SAA has taken the leadership role in the publication of books and articles related to business archives, other organizations have made significant contributions to the field. Of particular note is the special edition of *The Public Historian* published in 1981 that focused on the role of history in the business environment and the fine series of topical articles published in *The Business History Bulletin* distributed by the Center for the History of Business, Technology, and Society at the Hagley Museum and Library. The latter organization also sponsored a major conference on the theme of History and the Corporation in 1987.

While a review of the published literature is helpful in establishing a basic operational framework, personal contact with working archivists is even more important and can be accomplished through both formal and informal means. For over a decade The Society of American Archivists has sponsored an in-depth workshop on an annual basis, directed towards the business community, that focused on the essential elements of a sound archival program. Topics covered in this three to five day seminar include the basic archival functions of arrangement and description, appraisal, reference and access, and preservation. Additionally, at various times, segments have been included in the curriculum on marketing the archives, creating oral history, utilizing automation, developing security, working on preservation, preparing audio-visual records, securing management support, developing a first year plan, organizing records management, writing corporate histories, and using legal records.

Within the organizational structure of SAA, the Business Archives Section has been one of the most active committees of the society in advocating the expansion of business history and promoting a wider understanding and appreciation of business archives through a variety of publications and public programs. In addition to the publication of a biannual newsletter that reports news of current interest to business archivists, the section has sponsored a number of innovative projects including the publication of an advocacy brochure directed towards non-archival managers; suggested guidelines for corporations to consider in donating their records to outside institutions; guidelines for consultants to business on archival issues; long-term section planning; joint initiatives with the National Council on Public History and the International Council on Archives; and pro-active positive public relations programs on business archives.

All of the resources outlined above will provide invaluable data to the corporation that carefully reviews them and takes the time to apply scientific measurement techniques to them. In reality, most businesses employ the tried-and-true networking system of an information gathering whereby business relationships are employed to put prospective archival candidates directly in touch with active practitioners. While conventional wisdom asserts that successful archival models are transferable, there are a number of pitfalls that can ensnare the unsuspecting.

First and foremost, there is no single methodology that will apply equally well in all situations. Just as corporations pride themselves on their unique approaches to their mission statements, so do archival programs differ in their structure and service. The best and most practical approach is to observe the work products of other programs critically and to apply only those elements that fit comfortably into your specific environment.

Secondly, since the operational cost of the program is likely to be a critical factor in management's view of a potential archives operation, one should exercise great diligence in determining the "real" costs of operation. A general review of current business archives programs suggests a great disparity in their financial structures and budgetary practices. Miscalculations here can jeopardize both the archival program and the internal advocate.

The most difficult area to quantify is the cost of staffing. Archivists are professionals with special skills who differ from both librarians and records managers in terms of both training and approaches to work. In suggesting job grades and position classifications, it may be more useful to compare the job responsibilities of the archivist with other mid-level managers in the corporate structure than it would be to rate it against academic archivists or information specialist classifications that may exist in an internal position hierarchy.

Corporate archivists themselves are reluctant to disclose staff salary data, but informal surveys suggest that most business archivists who come to the job with outside experience will earn salaries in the high thirties to low forties. Other staff salaries and the benefit packages associated with them are determined by individual corporate practice.

As referenced earlier, operational expenses differ widely depending on the budgetary philosophy of the parent institution, but some monies will be required on an annual basis for the following: employee memberships and training; travel; books and magazine subscriptions; outside professional services (photography, exhibit design, etc.); data processing charges; archival supplies and equipment; telephone and telex charges; shipping and postage. Additionally, if the program is new, start-up costs for the physical conversion of space and its appointment with appropriate temperature and humidity controls can be significant.

Field visitations and information-sharing sessions with other archivists represent one of the most effective ways of structuring an archival program, but the judicious use of outside consultants may be the more appropriate avenue for those requiring long-term professional counsel. However, the retention of an outside consultant requires that the client has very specific objectives in place and is willing to shop for a qualified advisor who understands the uses of corporate records. While there are a number of fine consulting organizations, there are an equal number of unqualified individuals and groups who readily don the hat of "consulting archivist" but whose work falls far short of accepted standards.

Archival knowledge is a specialized field, but there is nothing mysterious about it. In hiring a consultant, one should approach the task in the same manner one would hire an exhibit designer, computer programmer, or public relations agency. The following procedures may be useful in making a reasoned choice:

1. Demand that the consultant have recognized credentials. Individual certification of archivists is now a reality within SAA, and any consultant should possess this minimum credential. Further, the Business Archives Section has drafted a list of recommended criteria for consultants that they will readily share with requestors. Factors in these guidelines include education, work experience, and professional involvement.
2. Request client lists and summaries of previous work projects from consultants. Talk to previous clients for their review of the finished work product.
3. Do not limit your consultant search to one consulting group or individual. Request a written proposal from a number of sources and follow up with personal interviews where required.
4. Check with other archivists from the business community regarding the reputation of consulting groups you are considering. The good guys are well known as well as the scoundrels.

As in any endeavor, pre-planning and a good basic familiarity with the subject matter will greatly enhance the probability of a successful program. The more targeted your objectives, the stronger the likelihood that management will endorse and support history as a viable corporate resource. Fortunately, there is an ample resource base to allow the uninitiated to successfully maneuver through the maze of complicated issues that characterize the archival world. Armed with the accumulated knowledge of nearly fifty years of corporate archival practice, and guided by the compasses of both formal and informal consultants, you will be in a position to make decisions that are theoretically well grounded and pragmatically oriented.

Frederick J. Stielow, formerly an associate professor with the School of Library and Information Science at Catholic University of America, where he taught in the areas of archives, automated systems, and information resources and records management, is currently director of the Armistad Archives in New Orleans. He has previously served as director of the HILS dual masters program at the University of Maryland and head of archives at the University of Southwestern Louisiana. Stielow earned a dual doctorate in American Studies and History from Indiana University (1977) and also has an MLS from the University of Rhode Island (1980). He is the author of The Management of Oral History Sound Archives *and the recently edited* Two Hundred Years of Catholic Record Keeping.*

CREDENTIALS FOR CORPORATE ARCHIVISTS: CHANGING PERSPECTIVES AND THE NEW PROFESSIONAL

Frederick J. Stielow

At the start of modern corporate archives in the 1940s, the selection criteria for archivists were rather simple. Formal archival education was all but non-existent in the United States; instead, newly appointed "archivists" learned their trade on-the-job with possible supplements from workshops. Corporate archivists were typically selected from the ranks of professional historians, or from soon-to-be-retired or semi-retired executives with an interest in the past. The archives themselves were often mere treasure chests for important memorabilia. Matters have now changed. Since the 1970s, two related forces have pushed for a clearer articulation of archival credentials: (1) the evolution of corporate information structures; and (2) the professionalization of archivists.

THE CHANGING NATURE OF CORPORATE INFORMATION

During the 1970s, corporate archives underwent something of a renaissance, and archivists often had the chance to expand their base to new information functions. Blockbuster media events helped stimulate an interest in archives and history, especially in those institutions that were coming to their own centennials. Another push came from the law. Beginning in the 1970s, the courts increasingly supported plaintiff's rights under discovery to corporate information. The absence of information due to shoddy or inconsistent record keeping has been deemed *prima facie* proof of guilt in numerous expensive judgments. Yet the courts also tended to support denial under disposition schedules from professionally run archives. Thus, the archives and archivist's abilities with records management and legal knowledge of retention schedules can become a defensive haven for corporations.

The information age was also influential. In the past, the supervision of the institutional information and the corporate memory was frequently ignored or left in the hands of untrained clerks and secretaries—a necessary evil buried within the overhead. Computers altered this pattern. The value of information and possible costs for the corporation were too great to ignore.

Beginning with computerization for financial records in data processing centers, the cutting edge of corporate information has passed to the integrated perspective of Management Information Systems (MIS) and Information Resources Management (IRM). The ideal is to treat information as a resource which can be enhanced for better performance and even for the production of new products. Archivists are likely experts to help in such development. Archives are pre-existing information nodes, and their holdings are major internal assets for promotional and publicity purposes, with added potential to strengthen employee identification with the corporation.

ARCHIVAL PROFESSIONALIZATION

Fortunately, modern archivists have the expanded credentials to work within the new corporate information environment. They should be judged as part of the developing wave of information professionals. They alone, however, have the specialized skills to handle the data of enduring value and build a reliable corporate memory. Indeed, without longitudinal and human-centered archival perspectives, corporate information tends to suffer from the tunnel vision of computer-centered information experts— who are often more interested in the technology than in managing information to its best purposes or preserving the corporate memory.

Archival training is now well suited to bringing a broad synthetic approach to corporate information structures. From a base in academic history, quasi-apprenticeship training, and limited workshop training, studies have expanded since the 1970s. The ideal is now graduate coursework in archives and automation from a university program in archival studies.

Several players were involved in this escalation of and campaign for archival credentials. On one hand, the National Endowment for the Humanities and National Historical Publications and Records Commission stimulated a number of new archives beginning in the 1970s. But these federal agencies also started to demand a degree of professional knowledge as a requisite for employ in their projects. On the other hand, universities turned to fill the training gap. Since many of the new archives were housed in university or other libraries, for example, schools of library and information science began to take an interest in archival training. Given the "job crunch" in teaching at the same time, history departments also started to look for related training areas for their students.

The key player, though, was the Society of American Archivists (SAA).

In the 1970s, a new self-consciousness and the recognition of the need for additional skills arose among the members of the SAA. Their vision transformed the SAA from an ineffective volunteer organization into a national professional association with a permanent staff to help promote professionalization and retrain practitioners through advanced workshops.

By 1977, SAA completed a major step toward heightened pre-appointment standards with the issuance of "Guidelines for Graduate Archival Education Programs." The document reflected the nature of archival education at the time: adjunct or practitioner led programs of study with a three-course master's level sequence of two archival theory courses and a practicum as the primary training venue.

Even those guidelines soon proved insufficient. Computerization and new information demands in the 1980s went beyond a concentration on stewardship and history and toward administrative services and information management. Archival education helped prepare the way for this shift with the addition of new courses. For example, records and preservation management were both recognized as basic training elements. Teaching even entered the international standards scene with MARC-AMC cataloging and the vagaries of OSI (open systems interconnection) communications model. Contemporary students may be exposed to relevant courses from general management and business theory to specialized offerings such as Archival Automation, Business Information Systems, Corporate History, IRM/MIS, Machine Readable Files, and Oral History.

SAA also helped lead with new *Guidelines for Graduate Archival Education* in 1988. Acknowledging the need for periodic revision, its authors called for a regular faculty director plus computer, library, and preservation facilities. A brief outline of the document is instructive on the basic knowledge elements one should expect from entering archivists in the 1990s:

A. The Nature of Information, Records, and Historical Documentation
    1. Origins and history of humanity's efforts at written and other forms of communication and data manipulation
    2. The development of record keeping systems and their effect on societies, organizations, and individuals
    3. The social and cultural utility of archives
B. Archives in Modern Society
    1. Origins and development of archival principles, methods, and institutions in the modern world
    2. The types and varieties of archival repositories and holdings
    3. The influence of related disciplines and fields on the archival profession
    4. The nature of the archival profession
C. Basic Archival Functions
    1. Appraisal and Acquisitions
    2. Arrangement and Description
    3. Preservation Management
    4. Reference and Access

     5. Advocacy and Outreach
D. Issues and Relationships that Affect Archival Functions
     1. Law and Ethics
     2. Automated Records and Techniques
     3. Inter-Institutional Cooperation
E. Managerial Functions
     1. Organizational Theory and Practice
     2. Program Planning
     3. Human Resources Management
     4. Resource Development
     5. Building and Facilities Maintenance

Perhaps a dozen programs around the United States and Canada now meet those requirements and may be found among the listings in SAA's *Education Directory*. Several of these approximate a full master's degree in archives. Although SAA has pursued formal accreditation for such programs, current economic and political realities make such a step unlikely for the near future.

SAA also has explored other areas for credentials. In 1979, its Business Archives Professional Affinity Group began a study of the requisite elements for a business archives. Those findings were sanctified by SAA and published as "Guidelines for Business Archives" in the Summer 1982 volume of *American Archivist*. More recently, other areas in SAA have been exploring the idea of certifying repositories for meeting archival standards in terms of personnel, policies, and facilities—but this is still in the discussion stages.

Responding to calls from personnel departments and others charged with selecting archivists, SAA also launched an effort toward the certification of individuals. Preliminary work began in 1984 and by 1989 the Academy of Certified Archivists (ACA) was ready for departure as an independent organization.

Entry to ACA was originally through petitioning and a demonstration of educational qualifications and experience, but now centers on a "practice-based" written examination. Approximately a quarter of SAA's membership was certified by 1991. And, although certification is not for everyone and many qualified archivists are not certified, it should stand as a significant factor in selecting archivists and consultants for a corporate environment.

On conclusion, the credentials vacuum has been shrunk. Those selecting modern corporate archivists can expect an impressive pedigree, which will continue to expand. Beyond the degrees and certification, archivists should have the historical abilities to identify and the archival skills to build and maintain an institution's documentary heritage. They need advanced technical and legal skills to control increasingly complicated and sensitive materials, but also the bureaucratic and interpersonal talents to implement and provide counsel from top management to the clerical level. Given such, the corporate archivist is a vital resource for the future development of truly effective corporate information structures.

Anne Millbrooke studied history at Boise State College and the University of Wisconsin-Madison before receiving a doctorate from the University of Pennsylvania. She has served as a Mellon Fellow at the American Philosophical Society, a Smithsonian Fellow at the Smithsonian Institution, an information specialist (historian) at the National Bureau of Standards, and as a program associate at the Connecticut Humanities Council. From 1981–1991, she worked for United Technologies Corporation, where she managed the Archives and Historical Resource Center, provided references services, served as a museum liaison for the company, and gave presentations to general and specific audiences inside and outside the corporation.

INTERNSHIPS:
AN EMPLOYER'S PERSPECTIVE

Anne Millbrooke

Academic credit. Work experience. Money. Curiosity. These are some of the motives students commonly cite when applying for an internship. The student is central to an internship, but the student's school and the student's employer are essential participants in a successful internship. The student provides the effort—that is, labor. The school provides academic preparation and imposes educational requirements. The employer provides supervision and assigns work. All contribute time, and, ideally, each meets an objective.

By definition, an internship is a program wherein a student can gain supervised and practical experience in a professional field. Internships are common to many professions. In medicine the internship is a postgraduate requirement. In teaching the internship is in the form of student teaching for employment at the elementary and secondary levels and in the form of the teaching assistantship for employment at the college level.

In many fields the internship has long been an educational option. The opportunity for a formal internship in archives, for example, began in 1939 when the National Archives provided internships in conjunction with an academic program at American University. By then, the newly organized Society of American Archivists had appointed a Committee on Education and Training that recognized the value of practice—including internships—in archival education. Later, 1944, the Society of American Archivists and the American Association for State and Local History formed a Joint Committee on Internships. In 1946, for a final example, New York University and Columbia University announced internships in business archives for graduate students taking a course in business history. Despite these early expressions of interest, the internship remained an occasionally used option.[1]

Today the internship is becoming an academic requirement in fields like archives and public history. The Society of American Archivists currently

Figure 1. Peter J. Capelotti, then a graduate student at the University of Rhode Island and now director of the Flying Boat Society, completed an internship at the Archives and Historical Resource Center of United Technologies Corporation in 1988. Shown here with a wind tunnel model of the Sikorsky S-38 aircraft, he processed Sikorsky flying boat records and wrote a historical report on the S-38 during his internship. *Courtesy of United Technologies Corporation.*

recommends a "practica" or "practical field experience," "practical work in an archival repository," as part of the graduate education of every archivist.[2] An internship meets this requirement. A few years ago a committee of the Organization of American Historians observed, "Internships are, of necessity, incorporated in virtually all the public history programs."[3] From the employer's point of view, this professional and academic trend increases the availability of students qualified for internships.

The United Technologies Archives and Historical Resource Center regularly employs students as interns with a variety of archival and historical assignments. From the start of the internship program in 1980 through 1989, thirty-five students earned both corporate salary and college credit for their work. They came from as far east as Rhode Island, as far west as California, as far north as Montana, and as far south as Georgia. They came from traditional history departments, public history programs, and archival training programs. They came to United Technologies for the internships, after which they returned to school or entered the job market.

United Technologies serves as more than merely a host of the student interns. In hiring a student, the corporation accepts responsibilities. Any employer becomes responsible to the student and to the school that sent the student. The employer must contribute time and expertise, give assignments and instruction, and provide supervision and evaluation. In return, the employer expects work to be done. What follows is one employer's perspective based on what has proven to be a successful internship program for all three participants—the students, their schools, and United Technologies, the employer.

United Technologies is a large, diversified, international corporation with divisions that date back to the mid-nineteenth century. Headquartered in Hartford, Connecticut, the corporation currently employs more than 185,000 people, operates more than three hundred plants, and maintains offices in more than sixty countries. Sales exceeded nineteen billion dollars in 1989. Products include Pratt & Whitney jet engines, Sikorsky helicopters, Hamilton Standard space suits, Otis elevators, Carrier air conditioners, and automotive components.

The corporation, then known as United Aircraft, established the United Aircraft Archives within the corporate library in 1957. A librarian devoted part-time to maintaining the historical collections that incidentally came to the library. In 1972 the corporation transferred the archives from the library to the communications department, and a long-time employee became the full-time archivist. Throughout the 1970s the archives collected records, mostly from the Pratt & Whitney division, the aircraft engine maker for which the long-time employee had worked. Fewer historical documents came from Sikorsky Aircraft, which made airplanes before entering the helicopter business, and Hamilton Standard, which started as a propeller manufacturer.

An aggressive acquisitions program in the 1970s transformed United Aircraft into United Technologies. The acquisitions brought diversification. Reflecting both the growth of the corporation and the growing demand from within the corporation for historical information, United Technologies renamed the Archives and Historical Resource Center in 1981, expanded the scope of the office to encompass the entire corporation, and recruited a professional archivist with academic training in the history of science and technology. The collections grew to include records of the acquired companies. Standard archival practices became office procedure.

The Archives and Historical Resource Center is the central repository for historical records from throughout the corporation. Currently, the office maintains over five thousand cubic feet of historical records: correspondence, technical drawings, advertisements, photographs, films, and other documents, as well as a historical library collection of twenty-five hundred volumes. Work in the joint archives and history office encompasses the full range of archival practices in collecting and maintaining historical documents for use by the corporation. Historical skills are necessary not only in the archival tasks of appraisal, arrangement, and description, but also in providing reference services and in doing historical research and writing.

Student interns supplement the regular staff; the relationship between interns and staff is complementary. Students bring enthusiasm, academic training, and a willingness to work. They work hard as a rule, and they produce concrete products. The Archives and Historical Resource Center accepts up to two interns at a time, usually one graduate student and one undergraduate—for a possible total of six interns per year. The actual number of student interns in any year is less. How much less depends upon the availability of good and appropriate students. "Good and appropriate" are qualities measured by the student's interests and background, by the school's recommendation, and by the work that needs to be done. At any time the archives has from zero to two interns.

The internship program began on a trial basis with one graduate program at one school. The exclusive arrangement broadened because of the limited number of students available from that school's program, the lack of interest demonstrated by some of the applicants from that school, and the receipt of unsolicited applications from students at other schools. Later the program opened to undergraduate students with the identification of large amounts of routine work unsuitable to the breadth and depth of experience offered graduate students.

The graduate internship program is open to any student who has completed a substantial portion of a master's degree program. The applicant should be willing to do both archival and historical work in a business setting. Applications are particularly welcome from students interested in the history of technology and in business history. Careful selection is crucial! Students with strong, academic history backgrounds have consistently performed the best, because, in part, archival skills are easier to teach at the corporate site than are research techniques, writing skills, and subject competency. An accurate and specific recommendation from the student's school helps determine whether an individual is appropriate for an internship at this office. Having no intern is better than having an inappropriate student consume limited staff time.

A flexible, written schedule is given to each student at the start of the internship, which normally lasts fifteen weeks. Assignments vary, but each intern is required to process and describe historical records following standard archival practice, to conduct research and write a historical report on an assigned topic, and to assist in reference activities. Given the large volume of work to be done, every assignment needs to be done correctly and completely the first and only time; there is no time to repeat work. Clear instructions and continual guidance are required from the employer. Weekly progress reports, written by the intern and discussed with the employer, provide regular opportunity to review the status of any project and of the internship as a whole.

Since the graduate internship constitutes full-time employment at, or almost at, entry level, students are given one to three days for professional activities which include attendance at a professional meeting. Each intern

SCHEDULE FOR DEBORAH KENNEDY, JANUARY 15–MAY 11, 1989*

Introduction—January 15, one day

Process employment papers, receive orientation information, review schedule, prepare for first assignment

Archival Project—January 16–February 2, three weeks plus three weeks flexible for a total of six weeks

Complete preservation microfilming projects; inspect Hamilton Standard and Pratt and Whitney microfilm, master and user copies; transform box-and-folder lists into roll-and-folder lists; compile roll lists; prepare narrative descriptions of the microfilmed collections; recommend disposition of hard copies of documents on film; file rolls of films, master copies separate from user copies

Historical Project—February 5–16, two weeks plus four weeks flexible for a total of six weeks

Prepare a historical report on the wartime employment of women by the various companies that are now a part of United Technologies; conduct research in primary and secondary documents on site; conduct research in outside libraries and archives as appropriate; prepare an outline (due Feb. 16), continue to do research; prepare a written draft of the report; revise the text; prepare a final report

Professional Activities—April 14, one day plus three days flexible for a total of four days

Attend the New England Archivists meeting at Bates College in Lewiston, Maine (April 14); tour the Northeast Document Conservation Center in Andover, Massachusetts (one day); and do other professional activities (two days)

Reference Services—Three days flexible

Conduct searches, assist researchers, respond to inquires

General Support—One week flexible

Provide assistance as assigned

Conclusion—May 9–11, three days

Clean up projects and write critical evaluation of internship

*Schedule is subject to change as opportunities and needs arise.

The internship is fifteen weeks, full-time; this seventeen-week schedule allows two weeks of unpaid vacation, scheduled for March 26–April 6.

is also required to tour a conservation laboratory, usually in conjunction with transferring historical documents for treatment. In addition, students are discouraged from taking courses concurrently with the internship. The couple of interns who did take courses on the side tended to identify themselves as students rather than as new professionals; they accepted less responsibility for their assignments: "What is required? What do I have to do?" was their focus, not "What can I do to produce the best results?"

Twenty graduate students have completed internships to date. They came from the University of Connecticut, University of California at Santa Barbara, Montana State University, Appalachian State University, State University of New York at Albany, University of Rhode Island, and University of Georgia. Each student had completed most of the requirements for a master's degree, and each anticipated a professional career in history, public history, or archives.

In the eyes of the corporation, the internship program is not a permanent program. Periodically, justification is required to continue the program. The most effective justification is what the students accomplish. All assignments are part of the on-going work of the Archives and Historical Resource Center, yet the corporation would close the program if it were seen as merely a source of cheap labor or as a way around hiring limits. In other words, the corporation recognizes the educational nature of an internship, while, of course, expecting a return on the investment.

All interns process historical records. They remove staples and other harmful fasteners from documents, flatten paper, deacidify documents as needed, weed duplicate documents from the files, place records in acid-free folders, label the folders, arrange and box the files, prepare detailed box-and-folder lists, and write narrative descriptions of the collections. Among the records processed by students are Pratt & Whitney service bulletins for commercial turbojet engines, general files from the chairman's office of Carrier Corporation, general manager's files from Sikorsky Aircraft and Hamilton Standard, reading files of program managers in several operating units, and photographic materials (prints and negatives) from throughout the corporation. The better interns participate in the appraisal of records, recommend approaches to arrangement, and annotate finding aids.

Each graduate intern prepares a historical report on an assigned subject; the assignment is based on the needs of the corporation, with consideration given to the student's interests. Students have written about wind tunnels at the corporate research laboratory, air conditioning in the textile industry, Sikorsky factories, Hamilton Standard engine and flight control systems, Pratt & Whitney sites, and Cloud Wampler's career as a Carrier executive. The writing assignment requires students to go beyond the stage of a term paper and to revise their drafts repeatedly for focus, readability, accuracy, completeness, and documentation—per editorial comments from the employer. Several reports became master's theses. One, about the corporation's Turbo Train program, appeared in a scholarly journal. All are used routinely by the corporation for executive briefings, public relations, and other purposes.

Interns sometimes rise to special occasions. The most extraordinary example of this involved four truckloads of wooden models that arrived unexpectedly one summer day. Two interns, one graduate student and one undergraduate, dropped their work in progress. They uncrated, washed, sorted, measured, identified, and listed the models, which the Sikorsky Engineering Department had used in water and wind tunnel tests from the 1920s to the 1960s. The senior intern finally supervised the transfer of the models to the Sikorsky division where they could be displayed. Both students then returned to their previous assignments.

The graduate internship provides practical, professional experience. In contrast, the undergraduate internship exposes students to professional work, but at the pre-professional or support level. Undergraduate internships are for a minimum of ten weeks, usually full-time during the summer or part-time during the school semester. Any part-term intern is required to work a minimum of one eight-hour day per week; additional time, including partial days, is optional. Students who worked only partial days spent too much time getting started and thereby produced too little in return for the corporate investment in staff time and effort. Undergraduate interns bring a willingness to learn and work, but no archival background, and often limited writing skills. The employer teaches all the skills necessary to complete any assignment.

Fifteen undergraduate students have completed internships. Most came from the University of Hartford, a local school, and the others came from Trinity College and St. Joseph College, also local schools, and Syracuse University. Most were history majors. All received recommendations from their respective history professors, whether or not they were history majors.

The undergraduate assignments involve mostly routine and time-consuming work associated with filing masses of historical documents or preparing documents for preservation microfilming. One student processed approximately twenty-five hundred photographs in a collection. The student removed the old photographs from three-ring binders, placed each photograph in an archival folder, labeled each folder in pencil, and arranged the foldered photographs numerically in archival boxes. Also, she made photocopies of the images for reference use. A different student prepared a Pratt & Whitney collection of reports for preservation microfilming. He removed all binders and fasteners, arranged the reports by report number, created and inserted target sheets, and compiled a list of the reports. Another intern inspected the microfilm and keyed the list of reports to the contents on the reels. As a rule, undergraduate students do not receive writing assignments as part of the internship. As an exception, one intern prepared a senior honors thesis on the history of automation at Pratt & Whitney factories.

Practical experience—on the job, not in the classroom—strengthens credentials and competency. An internship can offer that experience. One

measure of success is what interns do after the internship. Former graduate interns, for example, are now employed in professional positions. One
works for a state humanities council, another directs a not-for-profit
historical organization, a third is doing archival work for a history firm,
and another is managing a video history program. In addition, one is the
director of a county museum, another is the curator at a museum, one
works in a corporate archives, and another in a university archives. Most
have successfully pursued professional careers in the broad field of
history—the ultimate goal of both the students and their schools.

From the employer's point of view, success is measured by the value
of work completed by student interns. Records processed and indexed
remain accessible long after the intern is gone. Historical reports are
repeatedly pulled from the files for use. The professional network of the
employer is expanded to the schools that send students and to the young
people as they embark upon their careers. These are returns on the
employer's investment. One former student wrote of her internship, "I
came to realize that the corporate timetable does not follow the academic
pace." Given how true that is, bright and capable student interns provide
most welcome assistance.

NOTES

1. Regarding early archival training, see Karl L. Trevor, "The Organization and
   Status and Archival training in the United States," *American Archivist*, 11 (April
   1948): 154–163; and Jacqueline Goggin, "That We Shall Truly Deserve the Title
   of 'Profession': the Training and Education of Archivists, 1930–1960," *American
   Archivist*, 47 (Summer 1984): 243–254. See also Thomas C. Cochran, "Business
   Archival Internship," *American Archivist*, 9 (October 1946): 385–386.
2. "Society of American Archivists Guidelines for Graduate Archival Education
   Programs," *American Archivist* 51 (Summer 1988): 380–389.
3. Organization of American Historians, Committee on Public History, *Educating
   Historians for Business, a Guide for Departments of History* (Organization of American Historians, 1983), 17. The Organization of American Historians also
   discussed the importance of internships in its guides on *Historic Preservation*
   (1982), *Historical Editing* (1984), and *Teaching Public History to Undergraduates*
   (1984); the undergraduate guide lists the responsibilities of the student (intern),
   the faculty coordinator (school), and the field supervisor (employer). See also
   Robert Kelley, "On the Teaching of Public History," *Public Historian* 9 (Summer
   1987): 38–46; and Noel J. Stowe, "Developing a Public History Curriculum
   beyond the 1980s: Challenges and Foresight," *Public Historian*, 9 (Summer
   1987): 20–37. The perspective of the local historical society and guidelines for
   implementing an internship program are given in "Take a Turn with Interns,
   How to Set up an Internship at Your Society," *History News* 36 (March 1981):
   16–19.

For a biographical sketch of Nancy M. Merz, see her essay, "Starting An Archives," elsewhere in this book.

ARCHIVES AND THE ONE WORLD OF RECORDS

Nancy M. Merz

In 1955, Morris Radoff, then president of the Society of American Archivists (SAA), expressed his regret concerning the splintering of the records profession in a prophetic address entitled "What Should Bind Us Together."[1]

As Radoff surmised, the archives and records management professions developed separately. In the last few years, however, a growing number of archivists are making efforts to bridge the gap between themselves and other records professionals. Recognizing the interrelationship of the professions, they find it valuable to join AIIM and ARMA (the Association of Records Managers and Administrators); to read their publications; and to attend chapter meetings and seminars. Some archivists even become certified records managers.

Yet misunderstandings persist, and the old stereotypes, though dissolving, are far from gone. These views depict the archivists as serving the scholar and the records manager, and the information professional as serving the business community.

Indeed, the records management profession grew out of the archival profession. Confronted with the massive volume of 20th century documentation, archivists in the 1940s realized that they must become involved with records creation.[2] Eventually, records management developed into a distinct profession. To enhance their professional development, records managers formed their own professional association, just as an earlier generation of archivists disassociated themselves from the American Historical Association to form an autonomous professional organization more than five decades ago.[3]

The archival profession maintains close ties to the historical profession from which it developed. Ironically, that relationship hindered as well as helped the development of the archival profession since the image of the ivory tower academic rubbed off on the archivist. That lofty image, however, was transformed into a more lowly one: an archivist buried in the bowels of a library or governmental building, covered with dust and spiderwebs.[4]

In recent years, archivists have addressed this image problem. Meanwhile, our records colleagues, faced with their own image problem, began reversing their image some time ago. Records managers quickly adopted management practices and appropriate language, elevating records man-

Reprinted with permission from *INFORM: The Magazine of Information and Image Management.* April 1988.

agement to a professional status concerned with the total spectrum of recorded information, not just records storage. Records managers capitalized on the value of information in the modern world, stressing the importance of managing records as the method which transmits information in addition to earlier emphasis on the cost-effectiveness of records control.

Records managers initiated a certification program more than 10 years ago, less than 20 years after the founding of ARMA. Today, membership in the Institute of Certified Records Managers is recognized as having attained a certain level of professional knowledge and skill in records management and administration. In contrast, archivists were slow to adopt professional certification and are only now establishing a certification program, more than 50 years after the founding of SAA.

The archivists' reluctance to accept certification reinforced their dusty image. That image and the traditional emphasis on the unique qualities of archives helped isolate archivists. However, the records professions share common interests and concerns, especially in today's technological world. Records management textbooks and journal articles cover material familiar to most archivists: retrieval of information, questions of privacy, the Freedom of Information Act, and disaster planning and recovery. Information management publications address the subject of technology and its impact on records policies and procedures, a topic which preoccupies archivists as well.

Many records managers incorporate archival theory in their programs and make provision for archival records, at least in terms of scheduling and storage. Fewer archivists, however, seem to be aware of records management principles and their role in archival programs.

That situation is changing. Those of us who have crossed the line learn much from our records colleagues. Over 15 years ago, I began my career in a traditional archival position, primarily responsible for a collection of colonial manuscripts. Later, I joined the Texas State Library and worked with local government records, performing both archives and records management duties. Eventually I became a certified records manager (CRM), and recently spent several years establishing and operating a corporate archives for a multinational, technology-based corporation in Dallas.

The distance between colonial manuscripts and high tech is not as great as it first appears. In addition to 17th and 18th century manuscripts, the repository where I first worked had a large collection of unique microfilm of historical manuscripts. Consequently, I learned much about micrographics while there: microfilm storage, standards, duplication, and maintenance.

These experiences, along with information gathered from the National Micrographics Association (NMA) (as AIIM was known then), ARMA, and the American National Standards Institute (ANSI) were valuable in my later position with the Texas State Library. The Local Records staff of the Library advise cities and counties concerning microfilming practices and perform records management duties. In Texas, many county officials microfilmed records of short-term value, such as canceled checks; used negative film in office areas; and filmed vital records for preservation with no knowledge of silver halide or archival quality film. Courthouse and city hall basements, attics, and storerooms bulged with records. Many of the records are eaten by vermin, coated with dust, and damaged by water. Permanent records were buried amongst the others.

The Texas Local Records Department, later Division, recognized the interrelationship between archives and records management and actively encouraged and assisted local governments in developing records management programs in addition to transferring permanent records to the state. Regional depositories were established to preserve older permanent records and alleviate the current storage problem for local governments. The Local Records Division quickly realized that records transfer was not the solution to the problem, and that an integrated system which regulates records from creation to final disposition was needed. Consequently, the state developed both a county and a municipal records manual, listing legal retention periods and providing guidance on records management practices.

Records management activity focused on conducting inventories, performance appraisal, developing records schedules, advising on micrographics, and authorizing records destruction and the transfer of permanent records to an archives. This met the immediate needs of local governments faced with massive accumulations of paper records. However, the staff started to realize the impact of technology on records-keeping practices. For example, tax rolls, a permanent record, are on computer in most Texas counties, not just the large urban ones. Concerned about the future preservation of these records, we consoled ourselves with the fact that there was, in many cases, a paper printout but were uneasy with that thought, knowing that printouts were not the final solution to the problem.

Leaving my position with the state, I joined History Associates, Inc., to direct the establishment of a corporate archives for a multinational corporation. The task focused on locating, preserving, and making available the company's permanent records which had accumulated over a 50-year period. The company had a records center housing over 85,000 cubic feet of records but no records manager. It soon became clear that the company had a records storage program, not a records management program.

Once again, the immediate problem was a traditional one: the storage of paper records. Over 16 percent (14,000 cubic feet) of the records center material was designated as permanent. The archives staff reviewed computer lists of records with permanent and non-permanent value before starting the search for the company's archival records. Among the permanent records, we found general files, gas receipts, reference publications, expense reports, even a box of "archival air."

Although the company communicates via an electronic network, its electronic message system is primarily used to transmit routine information. The company is still very paper oriented and records generated in machine-readable form, targeted for permanent preservation, are also retained on paper. Despite this current practice, the archives staff realized the future implications of an electronic communications system. Concerned with the uncontrolled growth of both paper and electronic records, they encouraged the development of a records management program to work in concert with the archives program, and effectively implement creation-control policies and procedures.

TECHNOLOGY SHIFT

Technology, as it advances, always exacts a price. In solving one problem, it creates others. Archivists initially embraced microimaging technology, which was heralded as the solution to the immense storage problems of paper records and key to information retrieval. Archivists used microfilm as a preservation tool and computers to develop finding aids.

We now realize that the shift from paper to electronic records keeping has vast implications for all the records professions. Traditional approaches to archives and records management may not survive the technological revolution. And yet this same revolution has prompted variations in technology and systems we have used for some time.

Despite predictions to the contrary, the paperless office is not yet here and the volume of paper records is still a major problem in today's world. Although records will continue to be present in a variety of media, the percentage of records retained in machine-readable form will most definitely grow with each passing year. Billions and billions of bytes and bits are driving us to develop new policies and procedures for records creation, maintenance, destruction, and preservation.

Electronic document transmission is already a common practice in both business and government. Reports, correspondence, and other documents are transmitted via the computer, and archivists need to develop the means to ensure the preservation of those documents which should be retained. Traditionally involved at the end of a records' lifecycle, archivists cannot do this alone.

The ability to easily manipulate data on a computer, altering records with one stroke of the keyboard, puts the integrity of a document at risk. Disks and diskettes are continually erased and reused by office personnel. Magnetic media is sensitive to stray magnetic fields and can be unintentionally altered by such fields. Records of long term value must be identified at creation for they may not survive to the traditional appraisal stage, or appear on a records schedule, unless we ensure they are recorded on a stable medium.

Provisions must also be made to ensure use of records retained in machine readable form. The use of machine readable records depends on the availability and compatibility of both hardware and software. Documentation is necessary because data is randomly stored on disks.

In this new world of records, archivists must become more involved with records creation and maintenance. Managers, information managers, and systems managers must become more involved with records quality. Archivists, records managers, and information managers must work together to establish standards and procedures before electronic records become the primary media for maintaining the institutional memory. Archivists can no longer afford to work in isolation and must take a more active role, working with records and information managers to establish guidelines and educate office personnel regarding records creation and maintenance. All the professions should be involved with the purchase and use of information systems.

Currently, archivists are discussing documentation strategies—the plans to assure the documentation of an ongoing issue, function, subject, or activity.[5] To develop effective documentation strategies, archivists must work together with other records professionals. The design and implementation of these strategies also call for a cooperative effort on the part of archivists, records, information, and systems managers.

The technological revolution affecting all records professions gives us an opportunity to work together to design comprehensive records systems. A good example of such cooperation is the Archives and Records Information Coalition (ARIC), recently formed to serve as a mechanism for information exchange.[6] ARIC is composed of the Association of Records Managers and Administrators, the Association for Information and Image Management, the Society of American Archivists, the National Association of Archives and Records Administrators, the American Association for State and Local History, the National Archives and Records Administration, and the Library of Congress.

We are all concerned with the administration, management, and control of records and information—that concern is what binds us together. Technological advances are making it increasingly difficult to draw an arbitrary line between the functions of archives and records information management. The changing world of records is bringing us even closer together as we rely on each other's skills and knowledge to develop integrated records systems. The fifties witnessed the splintering of the records professions. The eighties, many of us hope, is the beginning of a *rapprochement*.

NOTES

1. Morris L. Radoff, "What Binds Us Together," *American Archivist* 19 (January 1956): 3–9.
2. Wilmer O. Maedke, Mary Robek, and Gerald F. Brown, *Information and Records Management*, 2nd ed. (Encino, Calif., 1981), 18–33.
3. William F. Birdsall, "The Two Sides of the Desk: The Archivist and the Historian, 1909–1935," *American Archivist* 38 (April 1975): 159–173.
4. Andrew Raymond and James M. O'Toole, "Up from the Basement: Archives, History, and Public Administration," *Georgia Archives* (Fall 1978): 18–31.
5. Larry Hackman and Joan Warnow-Blewett, "The Documentation Strategy Process: A Model and Case Study," *American Archivist* 50 (Winter 1987): 14.
6. Victoria Irons Walch, "Information Resources for Archivists and Records Administrators: A Report and Recommendations," National Association of Government Archivists and Records Administrators, 1987.

PART IV
THE USABLE PAST

THE USABLE PAST

The last segment of this book focuses on the value of the documents contained in corporate archives. Paper and electronic records, photographs, artifacts, and other materials can justify the cost of their maintenance only insofar as they can be used. A number of the selections in the preceding parts of the book have highlighted some of the more obvious uses of archival materials, while others have outlined strategies designed to keep the utility of a well-organized and accessible repository uppermost in the minds of decision makers. This final section centers on uses of corporate archives at once more subtle and more specialized.

Ten years ago, George David Smith and Laurence E. Steadman wrote a highly influential article in the *Harvard Business Review* on the role that history can play in the modern corporation. Based on their own extensive work in the field of corporate history, as well as a highly skilled digest of the experience of many others, this article presents a compelling case for its value to business organizations, whether used as a diagnostic tool to get at the root of stubborn problems or as a source of inspiration to motivate employees. While Smith and Steadman argue that history is an integral part of a corporation's culture and memory that can provide both a sense of continuity and identity, they remind us that recreating the past is not a simple task. It requires not only careful attention to the organization's significant historic records but also some understanding of the basic elements of thinking historically. Characterizing an organization's historical resources as a powerful managerial tool, this selection closes with a detailed series of questions designed to help companies provide their own answers on how best to make their history fully useful.

Spencer R. Weart of the American Institute of Physics outlines for us the unique problems of maintaining historical records in organizations oriented to scientific research. The development of new technologies and of new scientific discoveries is a long and complex process, he argues, and frequently requires quick access to accurate records. A complicating factor exists in the tendency of scientists to simplify procedures and discoveries, once confirmed, thereby running the danger of creating an erroneous, or at best misleading, version of events for future investigators. Additionally, researchers working on weapons or other highly sensitive technologies often have special security needs. A final problem for the care and use of scientific records is the need for the archivist/historian to have a good working understanding of the material in his or her care, an understanding more and more dependent on advanced education in one or another field of science. Weart closes by discussing some of the problems involved in making hiring decisions for archivists in research institutions and includes information on organizations that provide helpful services and advice in this field.

In an article written several years after his often quoted work on the value of business history, George David Smith takes a second look at the practice of this discipline in the corporate world and finds much that is troublesome. Arguing for a more professional approach on the part of both management and the historical community, he explores some of the problems that result from lack of intellectual rigor or a disregard for accuracy.

Smith also finds reason for optimism, however, in several recent commissioned histories which provide a good example of serving clients' needs while meeting the highest professional standards. Analyzing several major historical projects at corporations such as Citibank, John Deere, and AT&T, he concludes with a set of guidelines for managers considering such an effort.

*George David Smith is president of The Winthrop Group, Inc., in
Cambridge, Massachusetts, where he has consulted on corporate
strategy, structure, and culture since 1982. He also is Clinical
Professor of Economics at the Stern School of New York University
where he teaches in the M.B.A. and executive programs. He has
written in both scholarly and popular media about history and its
applications in business. His major works include* From Monopoly
to Competition: The Transformations of Alcoa, 1888–1986
(Cambridge University Press, 1988); Anatomy of a Business
Strategy: Bell, Western Electric, and the Origins of the
American Telephone Industry *(Johns Hopkins University Press,
1985). He holds a Ph.D. in history from Harvard University.*

*Laurence E. Steadman has been president of Steadman/Coles, Inc.,
since cofounding the firm in 1981. A Boston-based management
consulting firm serving a diversified Fortune 500 client roster,
S/CI's practice focuses on critical operating problems and strategy
implementation issues. S/CI's client work typically invokes an understanding of the historical and cultural antecedents of the corporation's current operational problems as a first step in dealing with
them. Steadman holds M.B.A. and D.B.A. degrees from the Harvard Business School and earned his AB in history from Oberlin
College.*

PRESENT VALUE OF
CORPORATE HISTORY

George David Smith
and Laurence E. Steadman

Planning the corporation's future should involve a careful look at its
past.

*Corporations, like individuals, have more than skeletons in their closets. They have
accumulated ways of doing things. And, like individuals, corporations may benefit
from the old ways of doing things but may also become unable to adapt during periods
of change. At these times, managers can look at the history of an organization to find
ways it adapted in the past.*

*A history is also useful as a diagnostic tool and as a way of calling up great moments
from the past to motivate employees in the present. A company's history contains its
heritage and traditions, which managers need to understand if they are to see the
present as part of a process rather than as a collection of accidental happenings.
Perceiving a company in this way can enhance a manager's ability to plan for the*

future. Managers need to learn how to develop historical resources and how to put them to use.

Rather than sophisticated planning systems and guidelines, what ultimately gives managers confidence in their decisions is their accumulated knowledge of the way things work—their experience. Out of their own sense of the past, managers necessarily formulate visions of the future. But frequently executives have to consider the experience of the organization, in which their own histories are limited. A more systematic and rigorous approach to the past is crucial if they are to achieve a sense of the corporate past greater than their own peculiar memories of it.

A history of the company is an important though generally unexploited corporate resource. It has many values extending well beyond the celebratory function of the conventional "company history," in either its publicity brochure or anniversary-book form.

Some companies, like Citicorp, AT&T, and Consolidated Edison, have commissioned scholarly historical research on strategy, structure, and the decision-making process that is useful to the companies' managers. For the most part, however, the problem with company history, to steal a phrase from Henry Ford, is that too much of it is more or less bunk.

Most histories are self-serving celebrations or sensational exposés, two sides of the same worn coin. And most managers we interviewed regard the histories that their companies have commissioned as amusing but not very useful. They see them as full of apocryphal anecdotes, burdened with pointless routine and detail, or too focused on some particular event to be of value. As H. Peers Brewer, a corporate planning vice president at Manufacturers Hanover Bank and an ardent reader of history, argues: most internally generated histories are "too superficial, too low in thematic content, and too low in their levels of abstraction" to be either useful to managers or trusted by historians.

Most company histories deal with the contents of a corporation's past, rather than with its essence. They should concentrate on the dynamic accumulation of past events and decisions that has abiding significance for the present and the future.

As part of a ten-year planning effort, for example, Citicorp treated its corporate character and long-term success not as static givens but as a historical process. It correctly recognized that the present is a moment in the past's trajectory into the future. Corporate history can be a way of thinking about the company, a way of comprehending why the present is what it is and what might be possible for the future.

Thinking historically about the company does not, however, necessarily result in a company's developing scholarly histories like Citicorp's or AT&T's. We studied several corporations to determine what types of historical investigation are the most useful and legitimate for a company's purposes. Although we mainly investigated large corporations, much of what we discuss applies to smaller companies of more limited resources as well. Once managers recognize the value of the corporate past, they can enhance their ability to diagnose problems, reassess policy, measure performance, and even direct change.

COPING WITH CHANGE

Some years ago, a large and successful technology-based company found itself at a strategic crossroad. Since World War II, the company had employed a decentralized management structure and a strategy of product diversification. It had increasingly relied on debt financing. By the late 1960s, for internal as well as environmental reasons, these characteristics had become dysfunctional. Unprofitable lines of business had developed, and the technological heart of the business exerted too little influence.

The company's top managers engaged a business historian to help them understand some of the long-term strategic and structural issues they would face correcting the trends of decentralization and diversification. One of the historian's more important tasks was to develop a corporatewide educational program to acquaint managers with the need for change.

The managers read cases on the company's history replete with stories of changing strategies, organizational innovations, and various management styles. The program presented data on the company's long-term financial policies, research and development, manufacturing output, and sales. The historian took care to distinguish the abiding from the transient characteristics of the business.

Managers learned that the organizational forms and management styles with which they had become familiar and comfortable were really impermanent and had, to a great extent, outlived their usefulness. They were reminded that decisions and structures are not absolute but adjust to changing circumstances. In the company's own pre-World War I corporate organization, they found an instructive analogy for the impending new order.

Business historians undertake several important jobs: first, to understand a company's history in great detail; second, to convey this history to present-day managers; and finally, to act as agents of change. For these functions the historian's training as scholar and teacher is essential. By stretching managers' awareness of the company beyond their immediate experiences, the historian enhances their ability to direct and cope with change.

HISTORY AS A DIAGNOSTIC TOOL

Managers at every level of the corporation, from the boardroom to the shop floor, have a need for a history of the company that is larger than their own experience. Indeed, an innovative manufacturer of consumer goods facing a serious labor relations problem in an extremely important plant made one of the most powerful managerial applications of historical thinking we have found. Founded 15 years earlier as a "model environment" for its workers, the plant had (after strong beginnings) suffered serious problems in morale, in relations between superiors and subordinates, and in productivity. According to one company executive, everyone remembered that in the 1960s the plant was well oiled and its employees ambitious and productive. "The intent was good, the structures were good, morale was high—but it went bad." By 1975 no one knew why.

An internal advisor quickly noticed that a certain potent wistfulness crept into people's voices when they spoke about the plant's early years. Suspecting that people were succumbing to the good-old-days syndrome, he thought he should get the facts about what really happened to de-mythologize the nostalgia. A social scientist who had no ax to grind was hired to construct a history of the plant.

Having little documentary evidence to work with, the social scientist used interviews with all the employees—sometimes singly, sometimes in groups. To thoroughly reconstruct the past and to establish a precise chronology of events, he anchored the employees' accounts on the measur-able and verifiable evolution of the plant's technology and its changing output volume. In consultation with the plant's management and hourly employees, he developed an objective account: a common history that was more than the sum of the particular memories of the people who had lived it.

The history revealed that during the years when the company was rapidly upgrading the technology, no one noticed incipient problems in operations. As the plant grew from a small, experimental, collegial shop into a larger, more routinized, hierarchical bureaucracy, it required a different kind of management. As new executives attempted to manage the new standardization and demands for heightened productivity, they made decisions that unwittingly violated hourly employees' long-held work habits and expectations about decision-making processes, standards of conduct, tasks, and relationships among employees on the plant floor.

While management failed to recognize the ways in which it had gradu-ally undermined employee trust and expectations, the hourly employees neither realized the sources of outside pressures on management nor under-stood them (although they indirectly experienced them). For instance, when division heads pushed for tighter controls to sustain successful operations, hourly employees couldn't see that increasing interdepart-mental competition for corporate resources induced the controls.

Eventually it became obvious that the organization and its products had grown old together. As its initial products reached the end of their life cycle, the plant had to compete with newer facilities making new-generation goods. When the plant shifted its operations toward more diverse industrial and commercial applications which required more strin-gent tolerances and shorter production runs, managers had to adapt existing technology. And as able and ambitious employees transferred to newer operations, it became increasingly difficult for plant managers to hold down unit costs. At the same time, they had little control over product or capital decisions.

Things were so bad that a new plant manager even encountered prob-lems getting labor and management to sit at the same table. When he finally succeeded, they began by studying the corporate history. Learning the plant's common history had a liberating effect on the employees. They began to understand management's problems and to gain a better sense of the economic and organizational realities of the company. Managers, in turn, began to see how employee trust had eroded, and they acknowledged the legitimacy of the employee's sense that their expectations and rights had somehow been violated.

Instead of pointing fingers at each other, people began to ask the basic question, "What happened?" After discussing answers, the parties agreed to work on solutions to their common problems. As a result, labor-management relations have vastly improved, information flows more easily from the top down, and employees more readily respond to work-related requests.

Using the original technology with some modifications, the plant is now a very strong generator of income, producing some of the highest-margin products of the company overall. And (according to one internal account) instead of seeing the plant as a dying organization, people now see it as a testing ground for new ideas and an exporter of talent to the rest of the corporation. A detailed case study of the plant's past has become required reading for new employees. According to one company executive, the understanding the company gained from the experience is being applied to a new overseas operation.

The current plant manager, an employee of the company for over a decade, contends that charting the plant's history gives people a sense of what has happened in "real time"—an experience of the company larger than their own participation in it or perceptions of it. Those involved thus came to understand the significance of events they had lived through, whose underlying meaning they had not sensed at the time.

HISTORY AS ANALOGY

While every organization develops its own peculiar history and culture, different organizations often face similar problems. The learning achieved by one is frequently transferable to another. The people in the foregoing example took this to heart, and benefits continue to accrue.

This transferability is, of course, the whole point of teaching business cases: many are often like short histories. But while we all acknowledge the value of business cases in an academic setting (where they become kinds of parables of instruction), not so many see that cases can also serve managers as episodes to illuminate organizational processes.

Corporate histories, especially histories of older companies with continuity in a single industry, often contain analogues to contemporary concerns that can illuminate durable truths and reveal lost lessons about the fundamental nature and operations of particular industries. In a 1955 study of the Singer Sewing Machine Company, for example, Andrew B. Jack noted two contemporary sets of problems that had strong analogues in the company's 19th century experience.

During the 1950s, Singer was using many of the techniques in marketing to certain foreign countries that it had applied a century before to domestic areas with a similar level of economic development. Moreover, certain contemporary problems Singer had in working with modern appliance dealers corresponded, amid strikingly parallel conditions of market growth and product development, to problems it had in the 1850s dealing with franchised agencies.[1]

History, of course, never repeats itself exactly, and it is dangerous to rely uncritically on the past to predict the future. Even so, lessons are there to be learned. Sometimes a history's relevance lies in pointing out the irrelevant. Sometimes finding out why and how watershed decisions were made reveals not only their latent significance or comparative value but also their pertinence to the present.

One company developed a marketing policy very early in its life for reasons that made eminent sense at the time. Over the years the policy assumed an inviolable stature as "the way we do business." On the ground that something inherent in the business demanded continuation of the status quo, managers defensively dismissed challenges to the policy from within the company as well as from customers.

A consideration of the historical context of the original decision revealed that it had been made under conditions—financial, legal, and technological—that no longer existed. The question then shifted to its proper place: not "Did the policy work in the past?" but "Is it relevant now and will it be useful later?"

HISTORY AS HERITAGE

Resurgent interest in corporate cultures has led sociologists, anthropologists, and other students of organizational behavior to serious study of the role traditions play in the life of a company. Every company, even a new one, has a heritage and a body of tradition. If the company's heritage is the whole of its discoverable history, then we can define tradition as the selective transmission of that heritage. In other words, tradition can be thought of as the company's surface memory—the folklore, ritual, and symbols that represent the company's sense of its origins, purpose, and identity over time. Company tradition is passed on formally through orientation programs, written histories, tangible symbols, and policies. It is also informally transmitted through stories and routines people accept as standard. All traditions are embedded in the past but alive in the present. For this reason, their history is vital.

As it does in all cultures, tradition plays an important role in maintaining culture. But corporate cultures are more circumscribed, more easily altered, more manageable than the cultures of society. Managers, moreover, have long been aware of the motivational benefits of corporate tradition. In a study of the oral tradition at Hewlett-Packard (a company only a generation old), an authority on corporate folklore explains how the retelling of a story about the "Nine-Day Fortnight" has become an informal but powerful vehicle for boosting employee morale.[2]

Ten years ago Hewlett-Packard avoided a mass layoff during an industrywide financial crisis by having everyone work only nine of every ten days and take a 10 percent cut in pay. This episode has become a tale which old-timers tell to ensure newcomers that Hewlett-Packard takes care of its own. Moreover, the attitude the story reflects is now the basis for management's actions during hard times. In an industry short on skilled and experienced people, employee loyalty is one of Hewlett-Packard's prized assets.

But as we have seen, traditions that maintain the status quo can become liabilities when changing times demand new approaches. For example, the historical benevolence of one major retailer toward its work force has evolved in ways that constrain the company's ability to compete. Too often it has retained indifferent workers while insufficiently distinguishing outstanding performers from the pack. According to one report, this traditional paternalism, rooted in an early company manifesto, may have cut into the company's profitability and ability to compete against energetic newcomers in its field.[3]

Understanding how corporate paternalism evolved at this retailer versus how it evolved at Hewlett-Packard might reveal ways in which companies can either build or hurt employee effectiveness.

Times of great change or devastating crisis also call traditions and long-standing habits into question. When corporate traditions are challenged, managers can consult the company's heritage, ask questions, and relate newly discovered or long-forgotten events to contemporary concerns.

A heritage is often broad enough to support multiple traditions, some of which the corporate consciousness brings to the surface or submerges according to changes in circumstance. For example, as AT&T moves from the "age of telephony" into the "age of information," market forces and political pressures have called into question the basic ethos of the company as a public service corporation. Competitive pressures have shaken its tradition of benign bureaucratic management (which had stayed essentially unchanged in a regulated environment for 60 years) to its core. New communication technologies, impending legislation, and changing markets have forced AT&T to develop a new breed of manager—more entrepreneurial, more competitive, and more attuned to the marketplace.

Also, since the mid-1970s AT&T has been reorganizing its structure from a function-oriented to a marketing-oriented organization. The effects of this reorganization are reverberating throughout the Bell System. A recent regulatory decision that AT&T should separate the regulated from the unregulated Bell System businesses and find appropriate organizational forms for each has put immense pressure on AT&T's management to change and adapt.

Speaking recently about the company's reorganization and the attendant shocks to AT&T's traditional value system, Chairman and CEO Charles Brown noted that the attempt to sustain the old service ethic with a "new spirit of venturesomeness . . . carries with it the risk of corporate schizophrenia. For, to put it mildly, not in all respects do compulsions of the marketplace match the public interest obligations of a regulated public utility." But, said Brown, AT&T must reconcile this apparent duality into a single corporate character, using its history and heritage as its "surest guide."

To put it another way, AT&T's problem is to manage the required change with a sense of continuity—a sense of staying true to itself that is especially important to a company with a long history and deep-seated traditions. "Sense of continuity," says Vice President and Assistant to the Chairman Alvin von Auw, "is the strongest influence on the decision-making process at AT&T." When top management formulates policy, it often consciously keys the policy to AT&T's traditions. An internal booklet on policy, replete with writings of AT&T chairmen and presidents, provides a starting-off point for new policy statements.

The historical research on AT&T currently under way confirms what the company's executives intuitively grasp—namely, that the company's heritage supports alternative traditions. As it entered the less regulated, more technologically explosive world of the 1980s, AT&T's managers were able to look back at the company's risk and entrepreneurial beginnings in an ill-defined market with a novel technology and learn a lot from previous encounters with heavy competition and the profound strategic and structural transformations that marked the company's history before it took its modern form in the 1920s.

THE DISCIPLINE OF THINKING HISTORICALLY

In the examples we've discussed, historical thinking was not undertaken in the detached removes of the university library or the scholar's study. It took place in the active life of the business, where managers applied it to practical problems in which they had a real and current stake.

In thinking historically, however, managers should follow *some* formal rules. History is, after all, a discipline and—like economics, psychology, or physics—has its own approaches, methodologies, and constraints. While professional historians concern themselves routinely with methodology as they strive to perfect their craft, we'll simply note a few key attributes of historical thinking that the manager should bear in mind. Studying history entails the ability to:

See and explain the flow of events as a process over time, not just a sequence of isolated happenings.

Approach the past with a sense of surprise—that is, regard events and decisions as uncertain and thus recapture them unaffected by their real outcomes.

Treat any part of the past on its own terms and in ways that would have been comprehensible to people of that period. (Our natural tendency is to distort the past by reading it in light of our own experiences, ideas, and values.)

Understand particular historical problems or episodes in their contemporary social, intellectual, political, and economic contexts.

In order to discriminate between good and bad historical data, it is especially important for managers studying corporate history to have a strong knowledge of contexts. Moreover, the available records may be scarce or idiosyncratic and the most relevant reasons for decisions may not have been recorded at all. Indeed, recreating the past is often a matter of intelligently plugging the gaps with well-reasoned historical judgment.

IMPORTANCE OF MEMORY

Historical judgment cannot be applied in a vacuum. Because memory is crucial, the preservation and management of the corporate memory are among the truly important (though often neglected) tasks of the modern corporation.

Every organization has a memory, even if it is little more than the body of anecdotes illustrating something about corporate life that is passed from one generation to the next. Even bureaucratic forms, simple routines of work, standards of dress and protocol, or styles and arrangements of furniture convey impressions of the past, the corporate culture, and the company's identity and purpose.

The best support for the corporate memory remains a well-preserved and easily retrieved record of events and decisions. Some corporations have undermined their ability to make sound decisions through careless destruction of critical records or simply inattention to old data. As Earl F. Cheit, dean of the school of business at Berkeley, recently noted: it is "ironic . . . that at a time when all American institutions are becoming sensitive to the need to think beyond the short run, the very store of knowledge that could contribute most to the development of a longer-term point of view is being weakened."[4] The tendencies toward mergers, acquisitions, and appointments of outside top managers and directors, plus greater reliance on oral communication, have all contributed to a weakening of corporate memory.

Compounding the problem are the "records management" programs that destroy records rather than discriminately preserve them. In their fear of increasing the risk of litigation, some managements have carried the spirit of records destruction to ludicrous extremes.

One large company cited for antitrust violations many years ago found that, during the course of the trial, its position was unexpectedly attacked on the basis of what it had regarded as an insignificant internal memorandum. The corporate response was to defend itself against future legal assaults by taking no minutes of high-level organization meetings.

The result was isolation and confusion. The company did not destroy merely its history of 50, 20, or years past; it destroyed its formal remembrance of yesterday. Managers quickly discovered they could not remember what had been agreed to or why or who had taken what positions on an issue. They lost their ability to reconstruct decisions, all for the sake of obviating unpredictable legal hassles.

Fortunately, many organizations are now systematically preserving significant records in the belief that the benefits outweigh the risks. Wells Fargo, Foremost-McKesson, Chase Manhattan Bank, AT&T, and the New York Stock Exchange are developing sophisticated, high-level archival programs. Wells Fargo, for instance, has a department of history staffed by professional historians, archivists, and curators.

Others, such as International Harvester, General Motors, Ford, Coca-Cola, and the Bank of America, already have splendid archives. Ironically, however, managers rarely tap archives for practical business applications. The problem, as one public relations executive told us, lies in getting top-level support to take what people ordinarily think of as "just a collection of dusty documents" and turn them into a "living resource."

Creating a living archive is not simply a case of preserving important economic, financial, and legal records or of enshrining formal statements of policy, strategy, and public relations. Correspondence, memoranda, recorded interviews, and even informal notes that might shed light on the decision-making processes of the organization must be available for study and analysis.

Peter Drucker has suggested four areas in which managing for the future requires careful assessment of the past: capital appropriations, personnel decisions, innovation, and analysis of strategies. Archives should be geared to the historical evaluation of the company's management and its ability to move from problems to decisions to desired outcomes.[5]

APPLICATIONS & WIDER SIGNIFICANCE

Historical thinking can enhance some concrete corporate tasks (see the table). These tasks range from public relations to corporate planning and include market research, legal support, and personnel.

Corporate Applications of Historical Research

Focus	Products of Research	Purpose
Corporate planning	Studies of the fundamental strategic and structural development of the company	To help avoid irrelevant or misguided trajectories into the future and to ensure that assumptions about the past and present are correctly based
	Case studies of corporate successes and failures suggesting effective and ineffective courses of past action and their determinants	
	Studies of specific past policies, strategies, or decisions to determine their relevance in current contexts	
	Studies of the causes and evolution of specific contemporary problems	

Corporate planning (continued)	Studies of the abiding and transient features of the corporate culture	
Management development	In-house publications or problems for acculturation of new employees Case studies for management training programs Resource materials for diagnosing organizational ills and for reorienting managers in times of change	To provide managers with an experience and knowledge of the company larger than their own
Marketing	Themes for advertising Development and maintenance of corporate and brand images Analysis of historical market entry into and exit from target communities	To help differentiate the company from its competitors, to authenticate advertising, and to support market planning efforts
Legal support	Assemblies of primary resources for legal research Determinations of facts in support of legal claims, positions, or briefs Briefings for attorneys as to the underlying social, political, and economic reasons for past events and decisions together with their specific causes and consequences. Especially valuable for antitrust or regulatory proceedings in which historical patterns and relationships loom large	To supplement the specialized legal resources of the company with expertise in either more general or more historically arcane research problems

The development of good corporate history has importance for historians as well. Lying at the heart of our technological, social, and economic development, the corporation has become a central institution of contemporary society. Well researched historical cases would not only broaden the base for business scholarship but also inform public policy. Policy is sometimes weak in historical understanding of the private corporation, its dynamics, and its long-term relationship to and impact on society.

At Citibank, historians look forward to preparing historically based arguments about the ways government controls have succeeded or failed in their industry. According to Harvard's Thomas McCraw, an expert on the history of regulation, business executives and regulators have a long way to go in sorting out successful from unsuccessful patterns of business regulation. Rhetoric too often substitutes for understanding.

Thus, at one level, good corporate history contains meaning through which the manager can relate his own experience and values to the larger life of the company. At another level, it relates the company's long-term role to the larger life of society.

PRESERVING THE CORPORATE MEMORY

The story is told that when David Rockefeller was preparing for a trip to China, he asked an assistant to go to the Chase Manhattan archives to find out something about the bank's early dealings in the Far East. When the assistant reported back that there *were* no archives, Rockefeller was astonished. An archival program was promptly begun.

When senior management decides to take stock of the company's historical resources, the first thing to consider is the potentially high value-added uses of the company history:

- At Citibank the payoffs are seen as related to the process of corporate planning.
- At Consolidated Edison management succession is being aided by a history of the recent period to provide a context for decision making.
- At Wells Fargo, which operates in an industry with relatively undifferentiated product offerings or service offerings, the corporate history is a powerful marketing and advertising tool that gives the bank a distinctive character.
- At Hewlett-Packard the history has been a vehicle for sustaining employee morale.
- At AT&T historical research illuminates organizational issues.
- At General Motors the company's history is used to support programs in management education.
- At the New York Stock Exchange the corporate history underwrites strong university and public relations programs.
- Elsewhere, professional historical research serves as an aid to corporate litigation, policy reviews, and even (as we discussed) labor-management relations.

Whatever applications the company's history may have, identifying and articulating them is the first step in making the company's historical resources coherent. To do this, management needs to ask the following questions:

- What is the state of our corporate memory? What records-management policies pertain to it? When did our historical resources and our policies governing them last undergo executive review?

- What has been written about the company? By whom? What is the general quality of such work? Does the public history of the company contain serious distortions or omissions?
- Does the company have a strong connection with the historical profession? What policies govern the response to legitimate scholarly interest in the company?
- Have historical accounts been published in such corporate publications as annual reports, house organs, and publicity pamphlets? How reliable or useful are these accounts?
- What historical records or resources do the company's various departments require? How, for example, is historical research for legal purposes conducted?
- Does the company have within it or connected to it experts who can organize, tap, and use the company's historical resources? Does the company have a professional archivist or (in smaller companies) professional archival advice? Does it maintain relations with professional historians who know how to find, assemble, and interpret historical data or train others to do these things at a parahistorical level?

Because archival organization and methodology and the contextual problems of dealing with the often scrappy remains of the past are complex and specialized, the last question is especially important.

Managers also need to consider how to preserve high-quality data for use in the future. While corporations have mastered recording of quantitative processes, such as financial reporting and accounting, they find it hard to maintain good records on the processes of management and decision making. Because the electronic age makes it possible to write instantly erasable memos, it is doubly important to have someone on board who thinks about how important problems, events, deliberations, and decisions can be preserved in the corporate memory.

Many companies are undertaking oral interviews with significant people, conducted by an expert who asks focused and probing questions. Perhaps more important, however, is the development of ongoing methods of recording and preserving important facts. Historians can help here.

And, finally, the company could develop programs that use a well-researched history. Some useful questions managers can ask are:

- How does the company communicate its history to new employees? What is the historical content of training programs or ongoing management seminars?
- Would it be useful for the company to have ongoing public relations activities based on its history? Should the company create a museum or open a library? Should the company create ties to universities, museums, historical societies, or other community agencies that might have an interest in its history?
- When major policy changes are debated at the senior level, does the history of existing policy inform that debate? Should histories of policies be prepared for ready access?

• Should histories of company strategies and other decisions be developed
  to assess the past performance of the corporation in qualitative as well as
  quantitative terms?
• Should histories of the company's experience with social and government pressures be prepared to aid responses to public policy debates?

Once a company takes the three basic steps toward making its history
useful—establishing the high value-added uses of the company history,
identifying and rationalizing its historical resources for current and future
use, and developing specific programs and studies—it will find that it has
acquired a powerful managerial tool. While we do not imagine that our
own enthusiasm alone will convince skeptics or convert ahistorical managers, we can at least suggest that executives take a preliminary look at
their corporate histories in terms of costs and benefits. If they do this
seriously and conscientiously, they can assess both. We are confident they
will find that the benefits dominate.

Notes

1. Andrew B. Jack, "The Channels of Distribution for Innnovation; The Sewing
   Machine Industry in America," *Explorations in Entrepreneurial History*, February 9, 1957, p. 113.
2. See *Dun's Review*, June 1980, p. 96. A working paper by Alan B. Wilkins,
   "Organizational Stories as Symbols Which Control the Organization," June
   1980, provides extended discussion of corporate folklore at Hewlett-Packard.
3. See *Business Week*, October 27, 1980, p. 148.
4. "How Quickly We Forget," *San Francisco Examiner-Chronicle*, November 23,
   1980.
5. See Peter Drucker, *Managing in Turbulent Times* (New York: Harper & Row,
   1980), pp. 68–71.

Spencer R. Weart is director of the Center for History of Physics at the American Institute of Physics in New York City. He holds the Ph.D. in Physics and Astrophysics from the University of Colorado, Boulder, and served for three years at the California Institute of Technology in the field of solar physics as a Fellow of the Mount Wilson and Palomar Observatories. Prior to assuming his present position, he pursued graduate studies in history at the University of California, Berkeley. Interested in the history of modern physics and allied sciences, he is the author of Scientists in Power, *a history of the development of nuclear weapons and reactors in France, and* Nuclear Fear: A History of Images.

HOW A RESEARCH ORGANIZATION CAN PUT THE PAST TO WORK

Spencer R. Weart

Nowhere is the inability to retrieve old documents as serious a problem as in a research laboratory. Fortunately, there are trained professionals available to help technical organizations set up the proper archives.

All good managers have a system for using their organization's history. For management must often answer demands for bits of the past: a patent lawyer wants to know where an idea came from, years ago; a government agency wants to know exactly where and how a toxic substance was disposed of; a senior officer wants to give a speech with some anecdotes about past successes. And management will make its demands, for example, when it tries to understand why one line of attack has worked well and another has always failed. A person's own memory and experience are not always enough to answer such calls, and wise managers seek out the collective memory and experience of their organization. That is history, and like everything else, there are efficient and inefficient ways to use history—with the inefficient ones all too often prevailing.

A tool every manager uses, well or poorly, is records management. Many of the questions that come up can be answered only with a piece of paper, written anywhere from a few days to a few decades ago. Every organization must have some sort of system for storing and finding those pieces of paper; indeed this paper memory is so essential that it is mostly taken for granted. Sometimes deficiencies are noticed, when that essential paper just can't be found. But there is a more common, more subtle problem, when people have troubles because they simply do not expect to have information from the past readily at hand.

Nowhere is the problem so serious as in a research laboratory. In other organizations, essential documents are easy to identify and save: personnel and financial records, for example, and the policy papers of top executives. But in science and technology, many other sorts of records may turn out to be vitally important. In some extreme situations, such as Stone & Webster faces in managing the records of the Clinch River Breeder Reactor, the implications of every decision are so great that governmental regulations require essentially every drawing and memo to be saved and indexed. Researchers themselves often feel that all sorts of files may someday be valuable, and squirrel them away; in some laboratories I have seen armies of filing cabinets that have not been opened for years.

The result may be needless expense (paperwork is surprisingly costly to store), and worse, despair when a needed document can't be found because it is buried in a sea of files. The solution is to have a records management program that weeds files, discarding year by year the ones no longer needed, winding up with the ones that it pays to keep permanently. Usually that is only 1–2 percent of all the records. This last, essential residue becomes the organization's archives—its collective memory, lasting long after the people who created it have retired.

It is this final step, the archives, that serves as a goal for the whole system. And so records management works best when done in close cooperation with somebody who has experience with archives and history. Fortunately, there is a professional community of people with exactly that sort of experience. A number of research organizations—Bell Laboratories, IBM, Du Pont, Lawrence Berkeley Laboratories, and others—have already used such professional help to set up archives. The benefits were often more than expected.

HOW HISTORY CAN HELP

For one thing, once there is somebody at hand who really knows the organization's history and documents, he or she can give all sorts of quick help. Some real-life examples: A patent lawsuit was answered with an old record showing that the tool in question was in use 40 years ago; a stockholder bothered by an article in his church magazine that accused the company of scandalous acts was armed with proof that the writer was taken in by a historical myth; a citation for the ceremony honoring a retiring employee was made complete and accurate enough to please all the old-timers; a television station seeking photographs of a famous laboratory founder got them in time for the evening broadcast. This suggests the sort of daily help that history can bring. Just as in research, so in management, an accumulation of little facts—if they are always accurate and accessible—can add up to a lot.

But management, like science and engineering, sometimes needs a broader look. That draws on a more subtle advantage of having historical and archival expertise on hand. All people make decisions on the basis of their experience, their ideas of the past. But what if ideas of the past are mistaken—can decisions be correct? That is no trivial question, for different people may give different stories of what happened years ago. When you check these stories against each other and against the documents, you will usually find that much of the past that people use is nothing but myth.

For example, when I interview physicists I often find that they like to simplify the way they made a discovery. Tending, as scientists do, to arrange things in logical patterns, they reshuffle past events to explain the way the discovery *should* have been made, the way it would be written up in a textbook. When people accept such versions of history—and buried within every decision is some version of the past, true or false—decisions rest on shaky foundations.

The full scale of the problem was pointed out by Harold Sharlin, who studied the uses of history in government technological agencies. Many agencies, he reported, ran into trouble when they misunderstood the long and complex histories of the technologies they were dealing with. They thought that their problem would be solved when they had an engineering solution, a way to dispose of nuclear wastes, a decentralized source of power, a supersonic airplane. They failed to see that such technologies could not stand on their own, but had to fit into a complex society. Better understanding of the history of, say, decentralized power—a matter of intense national debate for over a century—would at least have warned some managers of what they were getting into.[1] Understanding history on this scale of decades or more (the typical time-scale for diffusion of a research result into society) cannot be done from most manager's personal experience, but requires professional backup.

Recognizing the problem, a number of government organizations and some businesses have set up complete historical offices. The organization that gives closest attention to history is the one where hard decisions must be made most swiftly and accurately, with little but past experience for guidance: the U.S. Army. The army's solution, which is to maintain a staff of over 150 people writing histories of a high scholarly standard, obviously lies beyond the means of any research group. But if we consider the benefits that a group would reap if it could have a historical staff, we may begin to see how to get the benefits at a reasonable price.

I have already talked about two benefits: the everyday advantages of quick access to records, and the help to decision-making that comes from having accurate rather than mythical ideas of the past. There are other benefits of special value to research organizations.

Ever since the first industrial research laboratories were set up around the turn of the 20th century, managers have complained that they have a hard time recruiting and motivating the best people because of the pull of academic life. Not even high salaries always compensate for the recognition that university people get through publishing papers. As sociologists of science explain it, scientists are often motivated by the desire to make a contribution that is recognized by their peers, a contribution that is uniquely their own addition to the progress of humanity. It is something like having children: a bid for immortality.

Researchers do not often talk about these feelings. It was only after I found the issue coming up again and again, in the intimacy of oral history interviews, that I saw how strongly and deeply many people feel that the best reward for their work would be to have it remembered. Awards and citations, however appreciated, cannot by themselves satisfy this deep need. An organization that jettisons its traditions as excess baggage, forgetting what its past members struggled to achieve, would be a discouraging place to work. A program to preserve and use historical records solves the problem.

Relations with the public, too, can benefit from history. Most research groups have good reason to take pride in what they have done—past work that may only now be bearing fruit—and will gain the more the public knows their history. (The "public" in this case may include non-research branches of the organization.) Histories of scientific and engineering work have been used to great effect in exhibits, pamphlets, and entire books by many organizations, such as IBM, the National Bureau of Standards, Monsanto, and Imperial Chemical Industries.

Some organizations go in the opposite direction, saving almost no records past a few years, aside from patent-related documents. This has short-term advantages of economy, and it seems to solve fears that a "smoking gun" memo may someday turn up in the files to cause a legal or public relations disaster. But the practice has severe hidden costs. Throwing out records has some of the same effects on decision-making that cutting out pieces of a manager's memory would do. And it may remove precisely the documents needed to answer a lawsuit or a public relations crisis. At one time, the public tended to accept the good faith of business people, and still more of scientists. Documents were used mostly by opponents, sometimes out of context, as weapons to underline criticism that otherwise would not have been believed. Today, even when scientists are often disbelieved, a document may be the only tool an organization has to show its good record—provided the organization has kept the document and can find it. Studies of business often draw chiefly on records found in government agencies and courts of law; as MIT archivist Helen Samuels once remarked, that is like writing the history of a marriage from divorce court records.

HIRING A SPECIALIST

Decision-making support, company relations, public relations, access to documents to meet internal and external demands—how can an organization get all these benefits? Usually the first step would be to improve the records management program, with an archives as one goal. A good way to do this is to hire someone with archival and historical experience, and preferably with a specialty in history of modern science and technology. Often this person will need some clerical help for the first two or three years while working through the backlog of scattered old records. The cost in salaries and benefits for a three-year trial period, during which basic historical records would be sorted out and saved, would total perhaps $100,000 a year for a middle-sized establishment with a big backlog. This is not cheap, yet every place I know of that has established such archival control over its records would never go back to the old haphazard ways. Detailed studies show that the savings a well-organized archives can offer in managerial time and frustration, and in clearing out unneeded records, can make up for the expense.[2]

One fair-sized office with a desk, a large table, and a proper storage area will suffice to get a laboratory archives started. Typically, the first few months of work will liberate more space than that, just by cleaning out old records.

Some research organizations—for example The General Electric Research, Bell, Lawrence Livermore, and U.S. Naval Research laboratories—not only have an archives but a full-time archivist or historian of science. Smaller groups may settle for some professional advice in setting up archives, and occasional historical consulting to prepare speeches and reports for management, exhibits or pamphlets for the public, or an entire book for special occasions such as an anniversary. Some organizations may be able to get very inexpensive archival help by arranging to donate old records to a qualified nearby archives. Sometimes an organization can also have historical work done for free, if it attracts to its archives an academic historian who wants to do scholarly research.

In all these cases, of course, the organization will want to carefully check the scholar's qualifications before granting access, and may reserve the right to refuse permission to publish direct quotations from its records. An organization may also in fairness require that a copy of any writing that uses its records be sent to it for comments (not censorship) before publication. Of the many cases where a historian has been allowed free access to the records of a laboratory, I am not aware of a single time when the laboratory felt that the result was harmful; on the contrary, the results usually please everyone.

The way people feel about their history tells a lot about them. Those who are proud of what their organization has done well, want people to know about it—not just the public now, but above all future generations, the ones who will be most affected by today's research. And a person may well have a feeling of obligation, not only to the future but to the hardworking researchers and managers of the past, so that the story of their achievements is never lost.

WHERE TO GET HELP

Advice on setting up archival and historical programs for research organizations is available from several places, especially The Center for History of Physics at the American Institute of Physics, 335 East 45th Street, New York, New York 10017; the Charles Babbage Institute for the History of Information Processing at the University of Minnesota, 104 Walter Library, 117 Pleasant Street SE, Minneapolis, Minnesota 55455; and the Center for History of Electrical Engineering at 345 East 47th Street, New York, New York 10017. To find a professional archivist, see if a local university's library school has a course in archival management, or address the employment service of the Society of American Archivists, 330 S. Wells Street, Suite 810, Chicago, Illinois 60606. To find an historian, the first step would be to contact the history department at a local college or university, and the employment service of the American Historical Association, 400 A Street SE, Washington, DC 20003. For historians specializing in science and technology—particularly useful to research organizations—contact the Newsletter of the History of Science Society, 35 Dean Street, Worcester, Massachusetts 01609 or the Society for the History of Technology, Department of Social Sciences, Michigan Technological University, Houghton, Michigan 49931-1295.

NOTES

1. "What's Historical About Science and Technology Policy?" *The Public Historian* 2, No. 3 (1980): 26–28.
2. Reports on a study of Department of Energy national laboratories, with recommendations on archives, are available from the American Institute of Physics.

For extensive comments on a draft of this paper, I am grateful to Deirdre La Porte, Arthur Norberg, Helen Slotkin, Joan Warnow, and George Wise.

For a biographical sketch of George David Smith, see his essay, "Present Value of Corporate History," elsewhere in this book.

WHY COMPANIES CAN'T AFFORD TO IGNORE THE PAST

George David Smith

Company histories are usually handsome, always expensive, generally trivial, and sometimes counterproductive. They do little more than perpetuate vague memories, uncritical myths, and simplistic doctrines. Such histories, if read at all, can actually prove harmful by locking in or sanctifying the past, by reinforcing erroneous stereotypes, and by hardening resistance to change.

I come to this harsh judgment, I confess, with all the bias of a professional business historian. Relatively few of the hundreds of corporate histories with which I am familiar have been written by professionals in the field. Companies have generally preferred to entrust their histories to "name writers"—journalists, public-relations firms, or retired employees—rather than to professionals trained in historical research and analysis. Not surprisingly, this pains me, much in the way scientists or engineers might be chagrined were they to discover that industrial laboratories were hiring bicycle mechanics to do research and development in aerodynamics.

Then again, I must admit that not everything need be accomplished by experts. The Wright brothers, after all, *were* bicycle mechanics, and Alexander Graham Bell was a rank amateur "electrician" even by the standards of his time. Even today, scientific and corporate ventures come from surprising sources. (Witness, for instance, the Apple computer.) Wall Street is full of unschooled traders, and corporate chairs are filled with accomplished executives who did not learn their trade in graduate schools of business. I certainly have read some decent company histories by nonhistorians, even in areas I know something about. *Telephone*, by the journalist John Brooks, for example, is a nicely written and thoughtful overview of the history of AT&T; *Alcan* by Duncan C. Campbell, a former public-relations executive, is a competent narrative of one of the aluminum industry's most important firms.

In fact, compared with social scientists, historians have been slow to enter the arena of business. Many historians I know blame the corporate community for that. Corporations, they say, do not provide good access to their records and are not really serious about their histories, preferring to see themselves captured in glossy prints rather than definitive and truthful portraits. Some companies have actually suppressed manuscripts for which they had paid substantial sums of money. Others have placed far too burdensome restrictions on research, writing, and critical judgment. Most

Reprinted with permission of The Conference Board from *Conference Board* 70, May 1986.

professionals will avoid entering agreements that would allow that to happen, although not long ago, on the eve of the printing of the company history he wrote, a professor from the City University of New York complained to *The Wall Street Journal* that his client had prevented him from talking to potentially important people and had prohibited him from writing about certain matters. (I have always wondered what impact that kind of publicity must have had on the company's own perception of the value of his work.)

Indeed, historians commissioned by corporations to write company histories have not always done well by either the companies that have paid them or the standards of their profession. Allan Nevins's reputation as a distinguished American historian will not suffer by my observation that as a young, presumably hungry, man he once wrote an embarrassingly flimsy history of the Bank of New York, or that his other contract books fell short of the standards set by his more purely scholarly works. I will spare the living, but I should warn companies about entrusting their histories to those professionals whose interest in the commission is to supplement the income derived from their "really important" research.

There is a more fundamental problem that has retarded relations between business and the history profession. Among social scientists, historians are the most humanistic, and tend to be modest about making practical claims for their discipline. History does not aspire to predictive value as much as economics, sociology, and psychology do. Historians tend to be skeptical about humanity's ability to learn from the past, about the value of analogies, about the relationship between knowledge and decision-making. Even an applied practitioner, such as George Wise, who has just published a biography of Willis Whitney, the founder of General Electric's research laboratory, doubts that good history necessarily supports good decisions. Wise, who is employed by the R&D laboratories at General Electric, feels a tinge of guilt when he realizes that his own study of GE's early research has tended to justify the deemphasis on basic (as opposed to applied) research that has resulted from the merger between research and development in the 1970s. And in more fundamental terms, he wonders whether it is possible to draw a clear connection between historical insight and better business decisions.

This raises an interesting philosophical question, but such existential soul-searching can be carried too far. Business, as a practical matter, cannot afford to behave as if better knowledge of the past does not lead to more accurate assumptions on which plans for the future can be based. History does indeed have powerful diagnostic value; it also provides perspective and accounts for change. And at the very least, said Alonzo McDonald, CEO of the Avenir Group in a recent forum in the *Harvard Business Review*, history offers management an established set of facts from which managers make their decisions. It puts each problem in its own unique cultural and environmental contexts, says McDonald, and it provides the understanding that while "no two sets of circumstances are entirely identical," there is often "a general pattern which does repeat from setting to setting."

Many large American corporations, even those with catchy, futuristic names, such as Ameritech, Citicorp, Exxon, and Navistar, have roots that go back a century or more. Over the next several years, we will see increasing celebrations of corporate birthdays, marking the emergence of major companies (or at least their oldest parts) in the "big-business revolution" of the late 19th century. Already we are seeing a spate of corporate history books roll off the presses of book trade and vanity publishing houses, designed to encapsulate and perpetuate the triumphs of venerable enterprises. Much younger firms, 50, 25, even 10 years old, like to commemorate such milestones in some fashion; fair enough. A firm with a history of more than just a few years is a significant survival story in a world where most businesses fail quickly.

Writing history down, however, is a serious undertaking. It is a process by which stories, traditions, and customs take on the aura of reality and truth. It is something that companies, despite the considerable resources they may devote to it, do not, on the whole, do well. And that is a shame, because the history of any company is too important not to treat with the same respect for honesty, precision, and excellence that governs any other aspect of the enterprise.

A not uncommon version of the company history is the didactic compendium of stories about inspired founders, stalwart managers, dogged salesmen, brilliant scientists, inventive engineers, and, of course, dedicated workers, all of whom have pitched in like one big happy family to help the larger enterprise weather the slings and arrows of competition, government regulation, and outrageous fortune. Such histories quickly degenerate into hopelessly unbelievable texts and serve no useful purpose. Others are pointless renditions of dates, names, and facts, with no thematic structure or interpretation.

The time is ripe for a more professional approach to company history by companies and historians alike. The corporation has never enjoyed better public acceptance of its role as the central institution of social and economic development in an industrialized society, and its history is a matter of vital public interest. There is a real opportunity to bring the history of the corporation to the forefront of public relations. This is important, because the corporation, more than other institutions in our society, remains too generally perceived as a distant, monolithic entity. As it is, even the most sophisticated outsider's understanding of a business derives almost entirely from a reading of the public record, a poor substitute for informed research based on company sources. As Helen Samuels, the Massachusetts Institute of Technology's archivist, once quipped, learning about business through the public record is a lot like learning about marriage through the divorce-court proceedings. All you get is the bad news.

Good corporate history, in other words, can help explain the corporation for what it really is, a dynamic and complex culture of economic and social activity subject to all the pressures and problems of the larger community on whose behalf it conducts its business.

There are plenty of pragmatic, internal reasons for wanting a good company history. The typical corporation has a weak institutional memory. The ahistoricism of business literature, the accelerated mobility of management, and the increasing tendency toward reorganization have all served to diminish the already fragmentary memory of institutional life. The written company history is one way to provide contemporary management with vital information on past events and decisions that, no matter how distant, have shaped current circumstances and conditioned future options. It can provide a larger understanding of the business to all levels of the organization. And it can offer insights into the long-term evolution and prospects of the business to investors, regulators, and other important constituencies, whose responses to current and future corporate problems matter.

If such audiences are to be reached convincingly, the company history must be accurate, objective, and credible. The history must also convey the business, its technology, its markets, its people, and its dynamics in terms of larger political, economic, and cultural contexts. It must discriminate between the unique and common attributes of institutions, people, and events. It must deal with the enterprise in terms of its evolving strategies and structures. And it must provide an intelligent analysis of causes and effects, of intentions and outcomes over time. These are the things that professional historians are best trained to do: to study the process of change, to understand events and decisions in their proper contexts, to evaluate causes and effects, to make informed comparative judgments, and to assess the impact of the past on the present. All of this must be done on the basis of carefully documented evidence—the identification, location, and evaluation of which is itself a highly complex skill.

In the past 25 years, business has become more attractive to a small but growing body of historians as an exciting and legitimate field of inquiry. In 1962, the appearance of Alfred D. Chandler Jr.'s, *Strategy and Structure* marked a decisive shift in the quality and sophistication of business and company history, and opened up the field to a much higher plane of analysis. Chandler had been able to get open access to the records and managers of the companies he studied (it is often joked that his middle name, Dupont, didn't hurt), which enabled him to understand the corporation in far more complex terms than is possible through the public record. His richly detailed links between technology, markets, strategies, and corporate organization had a profound impact on an emerging generation of business historians.

Despite a growing number of business historians in the United States— from a few dozen a generation ago to a few hundred today—precious few have had much direct experience with business, or even with internal corporate records. That holds true for the even smaller group of technology historians, although surprisingly many of the latter had earlier careers in the engineering professions. Nevertheless, we are beginning to see histories of specific companies that are related to the best general trends in business and technology history.

But corporations cannot count on historians, left to their own devices, to formulate research problems or ask questions that might be of particular or compelling interest to the firms themselves. Margaret B. W. Graham's forthcoming book on research and development in the failure of video disks at RCA, and Leonard Reich's recent study of the origins of industrial laboratories at AT&T and GE (both from Cambridge University Press), have a lot to teach those companies about the internal dynamics of their technology development. There will probably be no better exploration of Kodak's formative strategies and structures than Reese Jenkins's *Images and Enterprise*. But all such academic histories are selective in the issues they address and in the periods they explore, and address the particular research concerns of the authors, which may or may not be of immediate interest to corporate management. Increasingly, companies that have historical questions they want answered are hiring professional historians to answer them.

There are some good recent cases in point. Histories of AT&T, Citibank, John Deere, and Norton have just appeared, signaling a new wave of commissioned histories that meet the precise needs of corporate clients while adhering to rigorous standards of historical research and writing. On the horizon are commissioned histories of Alcoa, Salomon Brothers, and Du Pont's research and development laboratory. These efforts vary in their subject matter, interpretative frameworks, and intended audiences, but they have in common a seriousness of purpose that far transcends the usual company history.

Citibank 1812–1970 is simply the best book on any American banking institution. It was written by two Citibank executives, Thomas F. Huertas and Harold van B. Cleveland. The latter is now retired, while Huertas, a Ph.D. in economics from the University of Chicago and a trained economic historian, is now assistant to the vice chairman for legal and external affairs at Citibank. His work on the history began in 1977 as a background study for the corporate strategy exercise that has since evolved into Citicorp's aggressive diversification of its financial activities, its campaign to loosen the regulatory structure, and the decentralization of its operations. Long before the history appeared, the findings of the historians and their team of researchers pointed toward some important conclusions.

When Huertas was asked to work on a plan for the investment banking area in 1979, the bank's long-term history showed that the institution's traditional strengths (before the separation of investment and commercial banking in the 1930s) lay in formulating global strategies that included both underdeveloped and industrialized countries. The history also validated a recent trend in Citibank's consumer strategy. In a highly regulated environment, which gave banks tight control over interest rates on deposits, a tendency had developed to view small customers as sources of funds for corporate loans. Recent developments in Citibank's consumer strategies hearkened back to a pre-Depression view of consumer banking as a business in its own right. This was a subtle point, perhaps, but it represented an important shift in thinking that was crucial to implementa-

tion of the new strategy. In all, the history pointed to a number of
correspondences between the bank's strategic and structural history in the
1920s and its contemporary developments; they were not identical, but
were at least helpful in thinking through the generic issues involved.

Huertas's research also prepared him for his recent tasks in corporate
strategy and regulation. He has been a persuasive advocate for the bank's
position on deregulation in both academic and public-policy forums,
drawing heavily on the strength and credibility of his credentials and
scholarly research. He likes to point out that in the process of writing the
book he learned that the issues leading to the strict regulatory codes of the
1930s (exemplified in most people's minds by the Glass-Steagall Act of
1933, which separated investment from commercial banking) were far
more complex and problematic than either policy-makers or bank executives have come to remember. A rigorous reexamination of that history,
from Citibank's point of view, justifies continuing attempts to achieve
regulatory reform in the changed environment for current-day financial
services.

The intended audiences for the Citibank history are primarily the
company's own management and employees, especially new recruits. It is
also expected to have important educational value for the banking community, regulators, and the business press. The book is just beginning to
receive wider circulation throughout the company. Those looking for war
stories and folksy biographical vignettes may be disappointed to find a
more technical, scholarly treatise. Huertas's hope is that the book will make
more "concrete" a common institutional memory that Citibank, with all its
recent structural dislocations, needs to reestablish.

My own reading of the book, which follows Chandler's approach to the
study of organizational reform as a necessary response to changing strategy, is that Citibank managers will find a strong rationale for the evolution
into decentralized operations, over which central corporate concerns will
focus on basic strategy, financial controls, credit policy, and management-
personnel development. The book may be a salutary reminder to an
institution that has had more than its share of turmoil (as well as success) in
recent years that the changes have a plausible basis in history.

AT&T has taken a very different approach to corporate history. Instead
of trying to achieve a sweeping view of the corporation in a single volume,
AT&T has just published three monographs on particular aspects of the
company's (and its industry's) business and technological development.
Robert W. Garnet, a Ph.D. in history who is employed by AT&T as a
manager in its archives and publications group, is author of *The Telephone
Enterprise*, which examines the process by which AT&T acquired and
organized its operating companies over a 30-year period, as administrative
systems were developed to manage a complex national enterprise. Neil H.
Wasserman's *From Invention to Innovation* is an intensive case study of the
implementation of the loading coil, a turn-of-the-century device that
greatly improved transmission over long-distance wires and through urban underground cables. Though I cannot vouch for the quality of my own
Anatomy of a Business Strategy, it attempts to outline the process by which a

History and the Art of Business Writing

A century ago, business executives said far more, using far less paper, than their modern counterparts. Business meetings were infrequent, and the telephone, originally conceived as an alternative message-carrier to the telegraph, was not yet a culturally established means by which people carried on lengthy conversations. Everything was written down.

Because latter-day managers wrote more, they had to write well. If not always elegant, business correspondence was at least clear, and it strove to develop ideas through carefully wrought sentences and to sustain ideas from one paragraph to the next. There were no bullets, no jargon, no simplistic outlines to make reading "easier," no shortcuts around thoughtful expression. It was not that time was any less precious then than now. There has never been a better example of succinct business writing than this oft-cited epistle:

> *Gentlemen:*
> *You have undertaken to cheat me. I won't sue you, for the law takes too long. I will ruin you.*
>> *Yours truly,*
>> *Cornelius Vanderbilt*

Where old business records have survived, historians can often reconstruct decisions with remarkable fullness. At AT&T's corporate archives one finds vividly detailed exchanges among that company's early managers, as they struggled to defend their patents, develop markets, fight competition, improve technology, integrate operations, and build administrative systems. The records reveal managers' thinking through false starts, half-formed ideas, good and bad experiences, and conflicting points of view. In handwritten notes, memos, and correspondence, they record decision-making as it actually happened. Today we tend more to record rationalizations of decisions after they are made.

The old records also reveal the predicaments and humanity of the business process. Consider the following from Thomas Sanders, the first treasurer of the Bell Telephone Enterprise, to Gardiner G. Hubbard, its first president, on March 5, 1878:

> *Mr. Cheever is I think sufficiently aware of our financial weakness not to make it desirable to any further enlighten him. I therefore went out of my way and told him a lie, that he might not think we were bankrupt. I hope I shall be pardoned for the number of highly colored statements I have been constantly obliged to make to keep up a semblance of financial solidity.*
>
> *We may and I trust will laugh over this one day but it is a sorry matter now. If I break down under it, deal gently with the widow and the fatherless!*

small group of patent holders developed strategies for vertical integration at a time when such a strategy was virtually untried and its results unknown. In each book, the telephone enterprise is viewed through a kind of distant mirror, reflecting a time when the business was unregulated, competition was a threat, technology was in flux, and entrepreneurship was at a premium.

If that sounds strangely contemporary, it is because the books are set in a time before the regulated Bell System monopoly, the image of which was long ingrained in the consciousness of every AT&T employee, regulator, customer, and adversary. Garnet explains that although the history of AT&T became unfashionable in the immediate wake of the divestiture, it is once again assuming some importance in the internal corporate culture and in the external image AT&T wants to project as it confronts its "upstart" rivals in newly competitive markets.

The three books launched an award-winning series on industry and business by the Johns Hopkins University Press. They strive to be more than just case histories in entrepreneurial enterprise. Garnet's book and mine are designed to bring different perspectives to bear on a complex process of industrial organization around evolving technical requirements, economic circumstances, and competitive strategies. They deal intensively with the decision-making process, based on internal records of remarkable detail.

Wasserman's study is an unusual attempt to examine the entire process of a technological innovation as it moved from the theoretical stage—pure science—through development, testing, production, and implementation in a systems environment. It is a case history primarily aimed at industrial laboratory scientists and engineers, and academic students of technology management. The other works are aimed primarily at the company's own management and at business and economic historians. The specificity of these audiences reflects part of AT&T's attitude that it is important to reach targeted groups in areas where opinion about the company is significantly shaped and where education about the business is likely to do the most good.

In that same spirit, AT&T is currently underwriting a book on the events and decision-making process leading up to the recent AT&T divestiture and the deregulation of the telecommunications industry. Peter Temin, an economic historian at MIT, working with Louis Galambos, a professor at Johns Hopkins, has interviewed numerous AT&T executives and outside authorities as well. This recent study has obvious relevance, Garnet points out, because the issues are still live. But even the more "ancient" histories are expected to offer insight into parts of the past that offer some useful parallels to current events and some basic lessons in telecommunications strategy, structure, and technology.

AT&T has been interested in looking intensively at problems of particular types in particular periods of its past, but it is also possible to take a slice of the corporate organization and examine it over a long period. At Du Pont, David A. Hounshell and John K. Smith are working on an extensive history of that company's industrial laboratory, exploring the nexus between research and corporate strategy. It will be a dense work, looking not only at the internal dynamics of technology and organization, but also at the external influences of public policy, war, antitrust, and competition. One intention of the history is "to examine more critically the traditional company myths that have shaped day-to-day responses," in order to enable the company to base its future R&D strategies on a more solid historical foundation. The intended audience, explains Hounshell, includes the company's own R&D personnel and extends to professional scholars, to policy-makers, and even to Du Pont's competitors.

Of the more conventional approach to company history, which looks at policies and strategies from a corporate perspective, Wayne G. Broehl Jr.'s *John Deere's Company* and Charles W. Cheape's *Norton Company* are two examples. The Norton history is very much an academic book aimed at sophisticated audiences, while the Deere history is more episodic and replete with illustrations, aimed apparently at a wider employee and industry audience.

Robert Sobel, whose remarkably prolific pen has churned out volumes on business history topics in the past 20 years, has just finished a history of Salomon Brothers for its 75th anniversary. In the past, Sobel has preferred to contract with publishers rather than directly with companies, but in this case he accepted a fixed fee administered by Salomon's public-relations representative. In turn, he has been granted open access to company records and personnel. Little is yet known about the substance of the book, which is due to appear soon, but the author does say that it is an attempt to set the firm in the large contexts of the financial development of Wall Street and to examine its responses over time to changing national and international markets. The firm naturally hopes for good public relations from the printing of its history, but the primary audiences are new recruits into the business, the financial press, and other firms in the financial industry. New members are seen as especially important to reach "in an environment where history is often understood as what happened five minutes ago."

Commissioning the professional business historian is no casual event and requires careful preparation. Even though my first engagement with a corporation was conducted on a handshake, which proved enough to give me free rein to conduct the research and writing as I saw fit, I do not recommend this. Instead, I offer some advice based on some of the best experience of corporate historians.

In the rare case of the internal company historian, it is important to find ways to isolate the historian from the pressures of employment as much as possible. In the Citibank case, the historians were buffered by the establishment of an advisory committee that included outside academicians of great stature, whose reading of the manuscript insured its scholarly integrity. The book, moreover, was submitted to a university press for publication, the standards for which required a blind outside reading by a critical scholar in the field. The history was cut off chronologically at 1970, predating the current generation of senior management, so as not to embroil the authors in possible conflict over interpretations of their superiors' performance. The result was a well-informed, deep, critical account of the bank's history by its uniquely situated authors.

Still, it takes a strong company employee to write an analytical company history, just as it takes a strong company management to commission a truly dispassionate book. In most cases, independent historians with some comparative-research experience are more plausible candidates. The Du Pont history, which has been contracted to outside scholars, also relies on an advisory committee. "Inside" members provide advice on technical and business points and help insure the accuracy of the manuscript. "Outside" experts provide peer professional critiques. This pattern has been followed elsewhere, including in my own current work at Alcoa, where a book of the history of the company began as a consulting study on the corporate culture and its impact on current strategy. There, too, the company prefers to publish in a front-rank university press, whose rigorous criteria for acceptance will eliminate doubts about the integrity of the work.

In planning the company history, companies should bear in mind the following guidelines. First, they should consider what audiences they need to reach. In some cases, significant audiences may be broadly defined to include employees, customers, and the general public. Often, however, the intended audience may be specialized or targeted groups, such as financial analysts, public-policy makers, professional or scientific communities, potential employees, or the company's own management and technical personnel. Choice of audience will largely dictate the form and content of the history.

Second, corporate histories may range from simple chronological narratives to focused studies of managerial or technical problems, events, and decisions. The most useful histories pose questions about the company's past that are related to the concerns of the intended audience. The answers should be investigated through a wide range of research, including a thorough examination of the historical context of the problems, decisions, or events in question.

Third, care must be taken to reconcile the needs of the company with professional standards of historical research. Companies must be prepared to guarantee open access to records and to personnel. In turn, the consulting historian must be prepared to concede the corporation's right to protect competitive secrets, a problem that applies mainly to very recent product and process information.

Fourth, the publication of a book involves many decisions about choices of press, copyrights, editorial review procedures, royalties, design, and distribution. Different books may have different production requirements and may be sold through different distribution channels.

Finally, companies must realize that the cost of producing a full-scale, professional history by an expert business historian is substantial, in the hundreds of thousands of dollars. The costs include the labor of the historian and associated research and support expenses. Costs will vary greatly with the scale, scope, format, and timing of the research, writing, and publication. One critical rule to remember is that histories that must be produced quickly are always more expensive than those that are done on a normal production cycle. Book projects may take years, not months, to complete. There are, however, many spin-off benefits from the research, which can be mined for a variety of other corporate uses in planning, public relations, and employee communications.

Not all companies may want or be able to afford a full-scale history for publication. There are a number of cases in which companies have found it useful to establish more discrete historical records of events and decisions, large and small. George Wise at General Electric spends part of his time preparing cases on research projects for future internal reference. Robert Garnet responds to all manner of requests for historical information from both inside and outside AT&T from his company's extensive archives. The Alcoa laboratories have recently produced a technical history of the research, development, and implementation of an important alloy for in-house education, recruiting, and public relations. Companies in varied industries, such as Boston Edison, R. H. Donnelley, General Motors, and Hewlett-Packard have employed historians to record and analyze important decisions, events, and experiments for internal proprietary uses. Wells Fargo Bank, which has the country's best business archives and the nation's only corporate history department (staffed by 100 professionals), taps the skills of its historians to support advertising, marketing, and litigation activities.

It is perhaps just another irony of history that as the functions of the modern corporation have become increasingly specialized—a phenomenon well documented by historians of business—the business historian is one of the last specialists to climb aboard. Business history remains an underdeveloped discipline, awaiting the development of more corporate data to expand our collective knowledge of the corporation. The corporation itself can use more insight into the dynamics of its past, if only to learn from its own experience. But the growing interest of historians in business and the corresponding awakening of corporations to the value of history bode well for the future of this largely uncultivated field. As that happens, both business and society will benefit.

APPENDIX A

**NATIONAL COUNCIL ON PUBLIC HISTORY
ETHICAL GUIDELINES**

I. **Historians' Relationship to Sources**

   A.   Historians work for the preservation, care, and accessibility of the historic record. The unity and integrity of historical record collections are the basis for interpreting the past.

   B.   Historians owe to their sources accurate reportage of all information relevant to the subject at hand.

   C.   Historians favor free and open access to historical research collections subject to the constraints of law and standard procedures of archives and records management.

II. **Historians' Relationship to Clients (Employers)**

   A.   Historians owe their employers the historical truth insofar as it can be determined from available sources.

   B.   Historians at all times respect the confidentiality of clients, employers, and students. Information gained through a professional relationship must be held inviolate, except when required by law, court, or administrative order.

   C.   Historians seek to perform professional quality work in accordance with their employment agreements or research contracts.

III. **Historians' Relationship with Colleagues**

   A.   Historians share knowledge and experience with other historians through professional activities and assist the professional growth of others with less training or experience.

   B.   Historians handle all matters of personnel, including hiring, promoting, pay adjustments and discipline, on the basis of merit without regard to race, color, religion, sex, national origin, physical handicap, age, or marital status.

   C.   When applying for employment or awards, historians submit applications and letters of recommendation which are accurate as to all pertinent details of education, experience, and accomplishment.

   D.   Historians give appropriate credit for work done by others.

IV. **Historians' Relationship with the Community**

   A.   Historians serve as advocates to protect the community's historical resources.

   B.   Historians work to promote a greater awareness of and appreciation for history in schools, business, voluntary organizations, and the community at large.

C. Historians represent historical research to the public in a responsible manner and should serve as advocates of economic or political interests only when such a position is consistent with objective historical truth.

V. Historians' Responsibility to the Canons of History

A. Historians are dedicated to truth. Flagrant manifestations of prejudice, distortions of data, or the use of deliberately misleading interpretations are anathema.

B. Historians in their work represent the past in all of its complexity.

Adopted April 1985

APPENDIX B

A CODE OF ETHICS FOR ARCHIVISTS

Archivists select, preserve, and make available documentary materials of long-term value that have lasting value to the organization or public that the archivist serves. Archivists perform their responsibilities in accordance with statutory authorization or institutional policy. They subscribe to a code of ethics based on sound archival principles and promote institutional and professional observance of these ethical and archival standards.

Archivists arrange transfers of records and acquire documentary materials of long-term value in accordance with their institutions' purposes, stated policies, and resources. They do not compete for acquisitions when competition would endanger the integrity or safety of documentary materials of long-term value, or solicit the records of an institution that has an established archives. They cooperate to ensure the preservation of materials in repositories where they will be adequately processed and effectively utilized.

Archivists negotiating with transferring officials or owners of documentary materials of long-term value seek fair decisions based on full consideration of authority to transfer, donate, or sell; financial arrangements and benefits; copyright; plans for processing; and conditions of access. Archivists discourage unreasonable restrictions on access or use, but may accept as a condition of acquisition clearly stated restrictions of limited duration and may occasionally suggest such restrictions to protect privacy. Archivists observe faithfully all agreements made at the time of transfer or acquisition.

Archivists establish intellectual control over their holdings by describing them in finding aids and guides to facilitate internal controls and access by users of the archives.

Archivists appraise documentary materials of long-term value with impartial judgment based on thorough knowledge of their institutions' administrative requirements or acquisitions policies. They maintain and protect the arrangement of documents and information transferred to their custody to protect its authenticity. Archivists protect the integrity of documentary materials of long-term value in their custody, guarding them against defacement, alteration, theft, and physical damage, and ensure that their evidentiary value is not impaired in the archival work of arrangement, description, preservation, and use. They cooperate with other archivists and law enforcement agencies in the apprehension and prosecution of thieves.

Archivists respect the privacy of individuals who created, or are the subjects of, documentary materials of long-term value, especially those who had no voice in the disposition of the materials. They neither reveal nor profit from information gained through work with restricted holdings.

Archivists answer courteously and with a spirit of helpfulness all reasonable inquiries about their holdings, and encourage use of them to the greatest extent compatible with institutional policies preservation of holdings, legal considerations, individual rights, donor agreements, and judicious use of archival resources. They explain pertinent restrictions to potential users, and apply them equitably.

Archivists endeavor to inform users of parallel research by others using the same materials, and, if the individuals concerned agree, supply each name to the other party.

As members of a community of scholars, archivists may engage in research, publication, and review of the writings of other scholars. If archivists use their institutions' holdings for personal research and publication, such practices should be approved by their employers and made known to others using the same holdings. Archivists who buy and sell manuscripts personally should not compete for acquisitions with their own repositories, should inform their employers of their collecting activities, and should prevserve complete records of personal acquisitions and sales.

Archivists avoid irresponsible criticism of other archivists or institutions and address complaints about professional or ethical conduct to the individual or institution concerned, or to a professional archival organization.

Archivists share knowledge and experience with other archivists through professional associations and cooperative activities and assist the professional growth of others with less training or experience. They are obligated by professional ethics to keep informed about standards of good practice and to follow the highest level possible in the administration of their institutions and collections. They have a professional responsibility to recognize the need for cooperative efforts and support the development and dissemination of professional standards and practices.

Archivists work for the best interests of their institutions and their profession and endeavor to reconcile any conflicts by encouraging adherence to archival standards and ethics.

Adopted by the Council of the Society of American Archivists, 1992.

APPENDIX C

CODE OF ETHICS
FOR
CERTIFIED RECORDS MANAGERS

Certified Records Managers should maintain high professional standards of conduct in the performance of their duties. This Code of Ethics is provided as a guide to professional conduct:

I.   Certified Records Managers have a professional responsibility to conduct themselves so that their good faith and integrity shall not be open to question. They will promote the highest possible records management standards.

II.   Certified Records Managers shall conform to existing laws and regulations covering the creation, maintenance, and disposition of recorded information, and shall never knowingly be parties to any illegal or improper activities relative thereto.

III.   Certified Records Managers shall be prudent in the use of information acquired in the course of their duties. They shall not use information, confidential or otherwise, for any personal gain or in a manner which would be detrimental to the welfare of others.

IV.   Certified Records Managers shall not accept gifts or other gratuities from clients, business associates, or suppliers as inducements to influence any procurements or decisions they may make.

V.   Certified Records Managers shall use all reasonable care to obtain factual evidence to support their opinion.

VI.   Certified Records Managers shall strive for continuing proficiency and effectiveness in their profession and shall contribute to further research, development, and education. It is their professional responsibility to encourage those interested in records management and offer assistance whenever possible to those who enter the profession and to those already in the profession.

Adopted by the Board of Regents of the Institute of Certified Records Managers
October 7, 1979

APPENDIX D

LIST OF ADDRESSES

American Association for State
and Local History
172 Second Avenue North
Suite 102
Nashville, TN 37201
Phone: (615) 255-2971

American Historical Association
400 A Street S.E.
Washington, DC 20003
Phone: (202) 544-2422

Association of Records Managers
and Administrators
4200 Somerset
Suite 215
Prairie Village, KS 66208
Phone: (913) 341-3808

National Center for the Study of
History
Rural Route 1
Box 679
Cornish, ME 04020-9726
Phone: (207) 637-2873

National Coordinating
Committee for the Promotion
of History
400 A Street S.E.
Washington, DC 20003
Phone: (202) 544–2422

National Council on Public
History
IUPUI
301 Cavanaugh Hall
425 University Boulevard
Indianapolis, IN 46202-5140
Phone: (317) 274-2716

Oral History Association
1093 Broxton Avenue, No. 720
Los Angeles, California 90024
Phone: (213) 825-0597

Organization of American
Historians
112 North Bryan Street
Bloomington, IN 47408
Phone: (812) 855-7311

Society of American Archivists
600 S. Federal
Suite 504
Chicago, IL 60605
Phone: (312) 922-0140

INDEX

Academy of Certified Archivists (ACA), 144

Access, to archives, 23, 63, 65, 77–79, 118, 120, 136; as archivist headache, 77–78; electronic, 121. *See also* Finding aids; Shelf lists

Advertising: archives as resource for, 3, 13, 14, 33, 81; banks and, 37–38; company history and, 173, 193; importance of, 37; oral-history input to, 68; Wells Fargo and, 37–38. *See also* Image, corporate; Marketing; Public relations

Aerospace Corporation, 8, 45–52

Air Force, U.S., Aerospace Corp. and, 46, 48

Alcan (Campbell), 183

Alcoa (Aluminum Company of America), 187, 192, 193

American Archivist, The, 136

American Association for State and Local History, 145, 157

American Historical Association, 63, 71, 182; archivist break from, 153

American Institute of Physics, 182n.2

American National Standards Institute (ANSI), 154

American Telephone and Telegraph. *See* AT&T

American University, 145

Anatomy of a Business Strategy (Smith), 189

Anderson, Harold P., 8, 37–44

Anheuser-Busch, Inc., 15, 130

Anniversaries, archives and corporate, 28, 58, 125, 130, 141, 164, 181

Annual reports, archives-reenforced, 15, 58

Appraisal, of archives-designated data, 17, 19, 23–24, 91–92, 120, 136; by interns, 150

Arbuckle, Ernest C., 38, 40

Archives: access to (*see* Access, to archives); arrangement of, 81–89, 91, 92, 136 (*see also* Texas Instruments Inc.); and corporate good will, 3; cost of maintaining (*see* Cost, as archives factor); as customer-service resource, 28, 33; government, 128 (*see also* National Archives and Records Administration); labor, 129; oral histories in, 76; physical aspects of, 32, 51–52; policies relative to, 50; qualifying for (*see* Appraisal, of archives-designated data); rationales for, 11, 23; restricted, 16–17 (*see also* Access, to archives); staffing of, 22, 125, 137–38, 147–48; urban, 129; uses of, 28, 36; value of, 1–3, 12, 13, 14, 131, 161, 178, 180–81, 182n.2. *See also* Archivists; Museums, company; Records management

Archives and Records Information Coalition (ARIC), 157

Archivist(s), 3–4, 10; and archives access, 77–79 (*see also* Access, to archives); certification of, 126, 138, 144, 154; education of, 125–26, 142–46 (*see also* Archivists, on-job training of; Interns, archives; United Technologies Corporation, Archives and Historial Resource Center of); historians and, 153; image of, 153, 154; and "information explosion," 115; maintenance/repair responsibilities of, 92; on-job training of, 126, 141, 151 (*see also* Interns, archives); as print editors, 33; as profession, 125; qualifications of, 12, 19, 137, 142 (*see also* Archivists, education of); and records managers, 65, 125, 126,

Management Information Systems
(MIS), 142, 143
Managing Business Archives, 136
MAPO (Disney div.), 54
MARC-AMC cataloging, 143
MARCON II, 25, 27
Marketing: archives as resource for, 3,
13, 33; of archives, 136; company
history and, 173, 193; importance
of, 37; oral histories and, 69. *See
also* Advertising; Public relations
Media: archives as resource for, 3, 15,
58, 178; TI archivists and, 32
Media Resource Library, TI's, 27
Memorabilia, corporate, 16
Memory: corporate, 171–76; optical,
116–18
Merchandise, Disney-inspired, 54
Mergers, corporate, 8, 63, 68, 69, 131;
and corporate memory, 171
Merryman, Sally L., 7, 8, 27–36, 63
Merz, Nancy M., 7–8, 21–25, 126,
153–57
Microchip. *See* Integrated circuit (IC)
Microfiche, 84
Microfilm, storage of, 19, 92, 151, 154,
156. *See also* Film(s); Microfiche
Microforms, data storage on, 1
Micrographics, 117, 154, 155
Microimaging, 156
Microphones, lapel, and oral-history
interviews, 73
Millbrooke, Anne, 126, 145–52
Mitre, 10
Mold, as archives enemy, 100
Monsanto, 180
Mooney, Philip F., 7, 9–20, 125, 135–39
Museums, company, 3, 8, 10, 129,
175; at TI, 28; Wells Fargo and, 14.
See also Exhibits, company; Wells
Fargo History Museums
Myth, "history" as, 179, 183

Nabisco Brands, Inc., 14
Naisbitt, John, 42
National Archives and Records
Administration, 125, 127–28, 145,
157

National Association of Archives and
Records Administrators, 157
National Bureau of Standards, 180
National Coordinating Committee for
the Promotion of History, 71
National Council on Public History,
71, 137
National Endowment for the
Humanities, 142
National Historical Publications and
Records Commission, 142
National Micrographics Association
(NMA), 154
Nationwide Insurance Co., 10
Naval Research Laboratory, U.S., 181
Neuenschwander, John, 74
Nevins, Allan, 184
Newsletter, SAA, 137
New York Life Insurance Co., 129
New York Stock Exchange, 10, 15,
171, 174
New York University, 145
Nisbet, Robert, 4
Nixon, Richard M., 73
Norton Company, 187, 191
Norton Company (Cheape), 191
Nostalgia, as corporate resource, 15–
16, 130
Nuclear power industry, records
management in, 178. *See also* Clinch
River Breeder Reactor
Numbering systems, archival, 64, 84,
85–89

Optical character recognition, 116
Optical disks, 1
Oral history, 4, 63, 67–76, 137, 143;
interviews for, 69–74, 175, 179
Oral History and the Law
(Neuenschwander), 74
Oral History Association, 63, 71
Organization of American Historians,
71, 146, 152n.3
Orientation, employee: archives as
resource in, 14, 32; at Disney, 56–
57; oral histories and, 68
OSI (open systems interconnection)
communications, 143